Special Forces Operator

For Guy and Caleb

Special Forces Operator

Serving with the
SAS and MRF

Robert W. Brown

PEN & SWORD
HISTORY

First published in Great Britain in 2021 by
Pen & Sword History
An imprint of
Pen & Sword Books Ltd
Yorkshire – Philadelphia

ISBN 978 1 52678 549 7

Typeset by Mac Style
Printed and bound in the UK by TJ Books Ltd,
Padstow, Cornwall.

Pen & Sword Books Limited incorporates the imprints of Atlas,
Archaeology, Aviation, Discovery, Family History, Fiction, History,
Maritime, Military, Military Classics, Politics, Select, Transport,
True Crime, Air World, Frontline Publishing, Leo Cooper, Remember
When, Seaforth Publishing, The Praetorian Press, Wharncliffe
Local History, Wharncliffe Transport, Wharncliffe True Crime
and White Owl.

For a complete list of Pen & Sword titles please contact

PEN & SWORD BOOKS LIMITED
47 Church Street, Barnsley, South Yorkshire, S70 2AS, England
E-mail: enquiries@pen-and-sword.co.uk
Website: www.pen-and-sword.co.uk

Or

PEN AND SWORD BOOKS
1950 Lawrence Rd, Havertown, PA 19083, USA
E-mail: Uspen-and-sword@casematepublishers.com
Website: www.penandswordbooks.com

Contents

I don't teach people to kill
I teach people to survive
If there is some killing
In the works, so be it
That's the nature of the beast

R.W. Brown (Special Forces)
Tugela valley, 1993/4

Author's Note

Names of some living persons have been changed to save embarrassment. Where I have used real names of deceased persons, I have listed them as killed in action (KIA), deceased or missing. The reason I have used the actual names of the dead is purely a matter of honour. I believe if one person remembers them, then a soldier never really dies. In forty years of operational service, the number of men I have known killed in action is high; I no longer count. Some are just names, others an image in my mind, and still others I have been close to and have known well. I think my life has been improved and the better for having known them. These men fought and died in distant lands, often in places not found on the map or in locations with names that most people would not be able to spell or pronounce.

In my profession as an operator, or professional soldier, I have signed documents such as Official Secrets Acts, as well as non-disclosure agreements, and I feel morally obliged to honour these commitments. To this end, I have given minimal operational procedures, operational names or call signs and at times have altered people's line functions. I have taken the liberty of masking the faces of soldiers I fought with purely for security reasons. Many went on to operate in other wars or still do. Some now have families or are still active against Muslim extremists in Iraq and Afghanistan and Africa. Our enemy today neither knows nor adheres to any protocols of war, being vengeful and vindictive in seeking out the weak, defenceless and vulnerable. The Special Forces operators I have known are brave and loyal, many being decorated soldiers. I omit their names not to dishonour them but as an accolade to their prowess. In the Second World War, when Adolf Hitler learned of the Special Air Service (SAS), it is reported that he said, 'These men are dangerous and to be shot if captured.' Today it is no less so; these men fought, lived and many died in a shadowy, secret world, so it is best they remain there in peace.

Stay safe.

Chapter 1

Beginnings

We are the Pilgrims, master; we shall go
Always a little further: it may be
Beyond the last blue mountain barred with snow,
Across that angry or that glimmering sea,
White on a throne or guarded in a cave
There lives a prophet who can
Understand why men were born: but surely we are brave
Who take the Golden Road to Samarkand

James Elroy Flecker, 'The Golden
Journey to Samarkand'

I think one could safely make the statement that I come from a military background. This utterance is not to imply that I live in a rambling house on a vast estate overlooking the shores of some loch surrounded by Highland heather, weather-beaten suits of armour and crusty old paintings of famous generals and war heroes. The best I could do for you in that regard would be to dredge up a couple of old former soldiers, these being my two grandfathers, now long dead. On my mother's side, Bryant or O'Bryant and on my father's Joe Brown. My grandfather on my mother's side was an Irish Catholic.

I think he dropped the O because of the troubles in Ireland, before joining the Guards. Yes, I have Fenian blood in my veins. He served in the Guards, first in the Anglo-Boer War and later on the Western Front. He was much disturbed when they would not let him have another go at 'Jerry' in the 1939–1945 war, or the 'rematch' as he put it. An unrepentant alcoholic and violent man when possessed with the 'demon drink', he would fight off two or three bobbies at a time. His other remarkable achievement was he drank the family into a Catholic poorhouse and orphanage. I have this information on proper authority, having had endless lectures about this particular demon from my mother, one of Bryant's many daughters.

I recall only ever meeting him once when he told me he possessed a pistol taken off a dead German soldier. Paddy, I will call him that as it's an acceptable name, I not knowing his first name. I think it is also less abrasive than calling grandfather by his surname. Paddy also disclosed having been shot in the back and left for dead in a tent; fortunately, someone saw movement and he was revived and lived. He had the luck of the Irish. Why an old man would tell such a story to a 5-year-old, I don't know. This meeting took place before my younger sister was born and she is six years my junior. This meeting resonated within my little head as I still remember it to this day.

Old Joe Brown took the Queen's Shilling. Being a Scot, he served in the Black Watch, also seeing action in the South African War and later the First World War. Yes, I also have Scottish blood coursing through my veins. Joe sired thirteen children. After the army, he became a rag-and-bone man, calling out in an incomprehensible and unclear singsong tone that only the initiated could understand, collecting old items of scrap or clothing that he would then sell on. He was also a cobbler; in fact, he was almost straight out of *Steptoe and Son*.

When funds allowed, he would drink copious amounts of rum and smoked twist tobacco, a dark tar-like substance that he cut with a knife before stuffing it into a pipe. He loved his horse, dogs and cart in that order, more than his thirteen children. He had more dogs than I could count. He died at 93 years of age or thereabouts, we think, as no one knew when he was born.

The interaction I had with either side was of short duration, and to say we were not a close family would be an understatement. I don't know the names of my mother's parents and only know that one grandfather was Irish and a thoroughly objectionable one when drunk, this being most of the time. So, my mother had a dislike of alcohol. Christmas was the exception with the occasional eggnog, possibly why only one visit took place with O'Bryant – the one meeting as already mentioned. I can recall Old Joe, father's father, but also my Grandmother Florence or Flo as everyone called her. She used to cuddle me, and I would disappear into her enormous bulk: Flo was a sizeable, cuddly woman. She had only one tooth that I could see, at the front of her mouth. Visits to them and reciprocal visits were few, but more than the one visit to the O'Bryants.

The only time I can recall my grandparents from my father's side coming to London was at Christmas. One Christmas, that's it. Travel from Derby to London in those days was an achievement. There were no highways as we know them today. The fastest means of transport would have been by train. At that time British Rail had been nationalized, and they were closing down many lines. I do recall an occasional visit to them. I spent hours playing with and stroking Old Joe's dogs, not having a dog of my own at that early age. Possibly the friendliest of the lot was a dirty old cocker spaniel, the rest being aloof or not used to little people. Old Joe would tell me to 'Watch that 'en' meaning a particular dog did not like children, with never a suggestion that the dog should move out of my way. If one snapped at me, he'd say in his broad accent, 'I told thee, leave dogs be.' His workshop was full of exciting junk that I was never allowed to return home with, as it was 'just old rubbish' but probably worth a fortune today. When he repaired shoes, or whatever task he was undertaking, he always had his tongue out, a habit that my father also had. What does one know about anyone after only a few brief visits?

My father, Alf Brown, was in the Royal Air Force in the Second World War and became an air gunner (Tail-end Charlie) flying 'Wimpys' – Wellington bombers. The air force never had any need for him to ride around on horseback. So there was little chance of him having his portrait painted straddling a horse. I believe being an air gunner at the rear end of a plane was a somewhat hazardous occupation in wartime: not giving them time to become famous, let alone time to have portraits painted or become a war hero, before being shot down or up or sent home gibbering, incomprehensible idiots. One should read *Catch 22* for an apt description of bomber crews.

The statement that I come from a military background does not rely on some vague, slender link to my grandfathers or my father. I have served in four regular units, as an active shoot-'em-up trigger-puller. When I mention four armies, it sounds as if I am incapable of keeping a job. Soldiering was my chosen profession. So, I am a professional Special Forces Operator, or soldier. I have been in eight theatres of conflict. Knowing this, one would think I have had or been given the opportunity to march in some jolly excellent victory parades. However, this is not so; I have not, not one.

Of course, this would imply that I have never been on the winning side. This is true and I hasten to add this is not my fault. I do think the blame must be laid squarely at the feet of politicians and generals. I did the best I could, having done a lot of shooting. One would assume not enough, as when the other side got to do the victory parades, there appeared to be a lot of them left. Plus, I never was a soldier of vital importance anyway. So I never got to make any world-shattering decisions on the stage of history. If my two grandfathers fought in the Anglo-Boer War and the world's bloodiest conflict, the Great War, one could assume that they were slow learners. Is this a reflection on me or my ability to understand dangerous situations and remove myself from them to a place of sanctuary and safety? It has to be a DNA thing.

I think my family was dysfunctional; never the less, mother always kept me clean, watered and fed – like the horses in the portraits that would have been painted had any one of us become famous. My father was a quiet man and did not engage me in conversation, or maybe he just didn't like me: why would you talk to someone you don't like? Some of the things I remember about my father: he was never a drinker. How could he be, having married one of O Bryant's daughters? He was married to the same woman, my mother, until the day he died, aged 93 and never once lifted his hand to her in all that time, although many doors did get slammed. I can also recall on specific dates he would raise a glass and with a middle-distance stare toast absent friends. My mother would always respond with, 'That's enough of that; we don't want any of that here.' Being young, I had no idea what that was all about and why we did not want it. I would only learn later in life what this meant. I never recall him being out of work. That counts for something in my way of reckoning. Alf was married to my mother until the day he died; that does not mean that she was the only wife. No, Alf was a lad in his younger days. I don't have a clue about the first wife, who she was, where she came from or where she went. For that historical stuff one has to have a family that eats together and communicates well.

I do know he had three children from his first wife, and for a time Eddy and the two girls Sheryl and Jenny came to stay with us, then disappeared much like their mother must have, and I had no idea where they went. The memories of this early part of my life are vague; they would be – I was only 3 years old. The bits I have pieced together are from when I met Jenny twenty years later when on leave from the Parachute Regiment. Eddy went into the British Army for a time; there was still national service in his younger days. I think he served in Suez or Cyprus – some crisis or other that the British always appeared to be having in the fifties and early sixties. They still do until they become too expensive to finance. Eddy was successful after he left the army, although I never really learned what he did.

My sister Jenny … well, Jenny was just Jenny, a lovely person. I found her by accident or by one of those unexplainable coincidences that sometimes takes place in our lives. I was in the 2nd Battalion, The British Parachute Regiment at the time. It was known as a Jock battalion because of the high number of Scots in the ranks. However, one of the lads was from London, a proper Cockney. I just mentioned I had family someplace in London and as the conversation unfolded, he listened and became more and more interested in what I was saying and the description I was giving. He then just blurted out, 'I know them!' He did too, so on our next leave he took me to her front door. I have pleasant memories and listened to many entertaining stories from her. I learned a lot, about skeletons. Jenny had lived in the same suburb in London and the same flat for years.

My side of the family has had a transient life; the chances of finding any of us would have been slim. Then maybe that was the object of the exercise. The reality is I was never to stay in any one home or country for more than two years until later in life and similarly at any one school. In the nine or ten years of schooling I had, I was in and out of nine different schools. The longest I stayed at any one school was at a private school that I had to leave when my father lost his business. The family moved from what I always thought of as the big house where I had spent my formative years before we became transient, much like Bedouins.

The 1950s was the first new decade after the Second World War and most of the world breathed a collective sigh of relief. Breathing in 1952 was difficult, as thousands who had survived the war died in the London smog of that year. The early 1950s, apart from the London smog, was a time of street parties held in celebration of Princess Elizabeth's coronation. All across Britain people had street parties and fancy-dress competitions, flags and bunting being put up all over the place. They forgot that only a short while ago, in living memory, they had twice put up the same flags and bunting to send fathers, husbands and sons off to war.

It was in the late fifties and early sixties the world was to witness a mass movement of people migrating to greener pastures. Men and women had come home from the Second World War to rebuild, men to marry widows who had lost husbands and widows to marry men who had survived. Those who did return changed forever. For the second time in twenty-two years young men served King and Country to return if God willed it, and like their fathers, many of them left as mere boys to return as cynical old men. Lives changed and homes were destroyed. Many returned to no family at all. Wives and mothers had evacuated their children never to reclaim them; husbands went off to war and survived but never returned, becoming part of this mass flux of people throughout the world. By the fifties, families had been reformed and established. More than a few saw no future for their children in the country they had fought for and became part of this wandering horde – many unable to live under the shadow of the Bomb and the threat of another war, this time, nuclear. Real or imagined, they just wanted to get away, and the war children who were now in their teens and twenties wondered what the big deal was all about; they were looking for new, freer life, whatever that was meant to mean. It always surprised me how England had an empire. Other than missionaries, traders, soldiers and of course convicts, it would appear everyone in England just wanted to stay at home. The opportunity for worldwide travel would increase for John Ploughboy with the advent of the Great War.

Finding Jenny who had lived in one place forever was not too complicated. She lived in a high-rise flat, as did most of London (other than the Queen who has a large garden), and of course, I did know her name – Jenny's name, not the Queen's. I was clueless where this suburb was in London, a city teeming with people.

I recall a story told me by Jenny as we sat and talked. My mother was somewhat set in her ways. When out shopping one day she came across Sheryl walking up the street with an American member of the US armed forces. Being just after the Second World War,

Europe had an oversupply of American soldiers waiting to be sent back home. My mother sprang into action, wielding her shopping bag much like a medieval weapon of war. Then, with the two of them within striking distance, she pounced as the two young hand-holders broke and ran, the GI in one direction and Sheryl in the other with my mother in pursuit, determined to brain this shameful, wanton teenager into the next world. From the telling of the story, I could imagine a determination to kill. The situation was aggravated by the fact the GI was black.

Sheryl later married a US sailor; apparently, she liked men in uniform (this one was white I think; his named was Westmorland something or other). Of these three siblings or half-siblings, I do have some memories.

From what I learned from Jenny and the little I can recall of my early years, my mother could be difficult. I was fascinated. I had found my English relatives, the missing part of my family. Jenny's stories had me absorbed as she told how they would go out on to Black Heath Common to watch the dogfights between the RAF Spits and the German Luftwaffe. Through their young eyes, the Battle of Britain must have been quite exciting even if all they could see were vapour trails and aircraft that looked like swallows. Jenny would laugh, saying 'Silly little buggers' then tell me how they used to put up their umbrellas to stop the shrapnel from falling on them.

At times, in my ignorance, I mistook the older men I worked with, including my father, as grumpy uncommunicative, miserable old sods. Character traits, which may have been the results of night after night sitting in the back of an aeroplane, wondering if you would get back for breakfast. Alternatively, sitting in a hole in the ground waiting for what? They're last-gasp, or that of a close cobber torn to bits by razor-sharp shards of metal, flying at an unimaginable speed. Men, laughing and reminiscing about some personal private joke, only they who share death can understand, gone now, gone forever. These men of my grandfathers' and father's generation, always amazed me. No personal reality tell-all TV shows revealing their suffering. I do recall Alf was a little disappointed that Bomber Command was never given a medal for their efforts in the war. He was pretty damning about a man called Winston. Bomber Command lost 57,000 killed out of 125,000 aircrew, that's a 46 per cent casualty rate. Include the wounded and POWs and it came to over 60 per cent casualty rate. Yes, most certainly 'to absent friends'. Alf had a right to be pissed with Winston. Alf before the war was a builder, an expert builder, City and Guilds no less. Strangely, he was not able to stay out of the war. I think he could have as builders were classed as essential services. Alternatively, maybe he enlisted before everyone started to drop bombs and blow up things, so builders were not needed then but air gunners were. At the end of the war, builders were most certainly needed. When Alf came out of the Royal Air Force, he started a profitable building company. All over Britain, massive rebuilding was needed. I can still remember the bomb sites in my childhood, and the war had been over six years. Food rationing only ended some years later, not that it had any impact on one as young as me. My father was a good builder and businessman, so the construction company of A.E. Brown & Sons took off like a homesick angel.

I had one sibling left after the other three had mysteriously disappeared – that was Keith. He was eighteen months older than me. Keith and I were fortunate enough to grow up in a large house because of Alf's building business doing well. Maybe everything looked big as I was so small. The term 'an agreeable early childhood' would be an apt description of my life, thanks to the success of the construction company. I should point out some credit must go to Adolf and the Luftwaffe for the time and effort they put in trying to level large parts of London. The house I called home consisted of four floors, including a basement where the offices were and an attic right at the top. Alf had converted the attic into a pigeon loft. He may have driven a Mark IV Jaguar and had the trappings of wealth, but Alf was still just a lad from Derby and a pigeon fancier at that.

He raced them. Pigeons always had a distinctive smell. I can even recall that smell today when not smelling cordite.

Vague memories, before my sister was born. I remember one of my father's labourers, indeed the only one I do remember. I could not remember when he had not been there, and he would be the last one I would see after all the others had gone. I use to watch him digging a trench, and his nose would start to run, at the same time he had a cigarette in his mouth, what they commonly called a fag. I would watch in childlike amazement as the drop from his nose would get longer and longer. I was sure it would drip onto his fag and put it out. Just as it was going to go drip, he would sniff and the drip would disappear back up his nose. I would sit and wait and, sure enough, down would come the drip … down, down, down, almost to the cigarette between his lips but a mighty sniff and it would be retrieved back up a nostril. Wouldn't you know it, his name was Drip. That's what everyone used to call him. He never stopped digging. Now that was an exercise in physics. He would also offer me a ciggy after he had rolled one before he lit it up. I learned the rolling of a fag was an art form that took much dexterity. If one became an expert, one could roll a fag using just one hand. Of course, this would take years of practice. I know all this because Drip told me, and I watched him roll a cigarette with one hand. He also smoked things called Woodbines or Woodies. After asking me if I'd like a smoke, he would say, 'Better not … stunt your growth.' He had thick white hair, almost silver, and a red face and he was big. He was from Ireland. I had no idea where that was, but he did tell me they had tiny people there. Not children but little people who lived down holes. I thought that was absolutely amazing. He called them the wee people. I believed in Father Christmas and the Tooth Fairy so no conflict there. All in all, it looked as if I was going to get through my childhood without too much drama.

I even went to a nice school. Nice is such a nebulous word and says nothing yet at the same time can say much. At lunchtime, we sat at a table that was the right size for four little people. The teachers sat at a large table, looking out at us. A bit like in Harry Potter minus the weird stuff. The tables had tablecloths and knives and forks and even real glasses for drinking. In those days, no one was paranoid about some 5-year-old smashing the glass in another pupil's face. I was civilized at a very early age.

The world I lived in consisted of people who worked for my father on site or drove trucks, as well as the secretary who came into the office, along with the char who cleaned out the budgie's cage, until she forgot to give it food and water and it died.

There was another world that I did not know of that one would call working-class or lower-income areas (a polite way of saying poor and broke). Mothers and fathers would get young children to go to the shops to get a bottle of milk, and a few rashers of bacon or a packet of fags for the old man, no drama at all. These children would sit outside on the pub steps waiting for Mum and Dad to send out a bottle of lemonade and a packet of crisps. I was the same age as many of these children. I never even knew what a pub was. In my world, we had bobbies who rode bikes or walked the beat. When they passed my father, they would tip their hat to him, and say, 'Morning guv'nor.' A police officer would step up to thugs and say, 'All right then, what's going on here?' or maybe, 'Come on lads, hand it over' and the thug would hand over a knife or some such weapon. Then the police officer would walk him to the police station without even handcuffing him. I did not know what evil people were or what a stranger was; in my world, none existed. In my little world, good always triumphed over evil. The bad, strange and unusual would come, but later.

Having said that, later was not to be a lifetime away. One day when Keith and I were walking home, we were attacked, not by some paedophile in a dirty raincoat, but by little people just slightly bigger and older than Keith and me. I must have been all of about five and a half, not much more. Keith chased them off and we picked up the remains of our books and made it home. That we altered our route showed prudence at an early age. I was, for some time, always looking over my shoulder. I don't know where our attackers came from, but they were different. They had holes in their clothes and their socks were always around their ankles, not friendly little people at all. Sometimes we had to make a run for it even when altering our route. After a time, we no longer saw them; maybe they grew up, or found slower prey. My world consisted of going to and from school using the same route. Other than a small detour to avoid the hostiles, I don't think I had any idea where I lived. This fact never entered my mind. I always had someone with me.

A series of events that would change my life forever took place sometime after my sixth birthday. Of course, I write or speak under correction. Jack the Lad, alias Alf Brown, was one for the ladies. I think somewhere he got involved with another man's wife. In today's permissive world, it would not be a problem, but then it was taboo, not to be mentioned publicly even if it did go on. Jack the Lad had been screwing the wrong lady, which had devastating consequences for business and family. My mother became extremely distressed. No one cared if I even went to school, a happening that did not bother me overly much. Then we were all packed off on holiday. So, Alf could sort out the business. No European trips for us; we were all bundled off to a place called Butlin's Holiday Camp. We stayed in some old army-style huts. The weather, let's say British, swept everything away in a big storm.

We were all back home two weeks later. The house was still there, but there had been a change. The first thing that went was the big black Mark IV Jag. I had no idea it was a Mark IV Jaguar; all I knew was it had large headlights, and the seats were, well, nice. The office lady and the desks and other equipment had gone. Was it the secretary or someone else who had thrown themself under a London tube train? Never to be seen again. At my tender age, I could not understand who it was that went under the train.

Sometimes people did fall under trains. When told about this, as children, we were always admonished with 'That will show you to be careful when near trains.' I suppose I was meant to retain this train information and the dangers thereof for future reference. Also, such wisdom as don't play with matches, another item I had no access to at that age.

I did notice Drip and my father talking in low voices on the odd occasion. I did miss the great heaps of sand that I use to jump and play in. All this vanished along with the car. When we had the Jag Alf and I would take secret trips, to go and see an old air force friend or a businessperson in a place called Wapping. Even that came to an end. No more stopping off at a workmen's café to be handed a crusty bread roll, stuffed with thick slices of yellow cheese along with a mug of sweet tea that was so big that people kept looking at me and asking if I was all right, and could I manage.

I always remembered Wapping – such a strange-sounding name. It was right by the river, the Thames. There were some old bombed-out buildings still left from the war, or bits of them. Most now levelled out. All that was left was an open space where a house had once sat, and a family had lived. Though the war had been over for some time, you could still find bomb sites. It was a place that had washing lines stretching from window to window. The walls were dirty, coated with black soot or grit. Alf would tell me to wait in the car as he disappeared into one of the grey-looking buildings. A short time later, an older boy, maybe 8 or 9 years old with holes in his sweater or pullover as they called it in England would come out. I would open the car door, and off we would go to play on the bomb sites or go down next to the river and throw stones into the water. There were places called slipways, long sloping driveways down to the river or just ending at the black mud if the river was low. You could find the most mysterious objects when the river was low. Old bottles and Wellington boots that made a sucking noise when you pulled them out of the black sticky mud. Broken crates with strange names painted on them.

I would ask my older friend, 'Can we go down the slipways?'

'Best not; you'll get muddy and dirty.'

That was the sum total of our conversation: having him telling me not to do things as it was dangerous, or I would get dirty, and he would get into trouble, or cop it. I recall he had the most amazing red hair and freckles all over his face, and long slender fingers and pale white hands. He always had the same clothes on whenever I saw him and shoes with no socks. I thought that was a fantastic idea. If you wanted to go down into the mud, you only had to remove the shoes and not worry about the socks getting wet or lost. He never allowed me to do this, saying, 'If you get wet from this water, you will have to go to the hospital and have jabs from the doctor.' I still thought it was a good idea to have shoes with no socks.

Sometimes we would descend steep steps that went right down to the water's edge. The walls and steps were made from sizeable hand-cut stone blocks with a green slime coating over them. If one touched the walls, the slime would come off onto your hands or clothes. One day my nameless friend was in a talkative mood. He told me that the green stuff was from the stone blocks always being wet, and you could see how high the tide had come up by the marks left on them. The line of green stuff came well above my head, and I wondered how long we should stay down there. Then I asked him what his father did when he was in the air force with my father.

'Don't know, don't know where my dad is; ain't got a dad, have I. Your dad comes to see my mum.' Then he went silent.

After that, we never had a conversation other than 'Don't, you're going to get dirty and I won't half cop it,' and the inevitable 'We best be going back now.' He never had a watch, and I always wondered how he knew it was time to get back. Maybe he counted the stones he skipped across the river. If that was the case, he must have spent lots of time throwing stones into the river because we always got back at the right time. The outings stopped once the car and everything else went. No more spins or crusty rolls that left flakes of crunchy bread rolling down the front of my sweater that I had to brush off before we went home. From that time on, I can never remember my father going anywhere by himself other than work. Irene was not going to let Alf out of her sight for more than a heartbeat at a time.

I was taken by my parents miles away from the big house to a dirty old dwelling in the south of London called a three-up and three-down. When I first walked into its dingy interior, I just cut and ran towards what looked like the only safe way out: light from the front door. The place looked as though Jack the Ripper was in residence. Or Oliver Twist had been laid to rest under the dirty floorboards. This was my new home. Who knew what dangers lurked in the shadows and in the mind of a 7-year-old? Besides, it smelt like something that I had never detected before: damp and mildew, possibly even stale cat pee. Welcome to the real world, squire. Every door had a broken or filthy door handle that did not work. A slow transition from an orderly privileged life was taking place. Cell-like rooms overlooked the street at the front, the back on to a garden that was no garden at all. It was, in fact, a yard in every sense of the word. At the far end was an old wooden gate that opened out onto a lane. The yard itself was barren, never having seen the sun. I think the term yard explains it admirably: the ground had been pounded flat and hard from people coming and going over the years through the gate leading from the lane to the back door. Behind the back door stood the scullery, it being another small room where one had the 'Friday bath night' using a large tin bath that hung by a nail on the wall waiting for its baptismal service every seventh day. My new room was just the right size to fit a set of bunkbeds in; Keith and I would share. It had no hanging space other than some nails hammered into the door as hooks.

Once renovated and made habitable by Alf the errant builder, a task that took some time, my mother let out rooms or beds to lodgers. The posh word would be a guesthouse. Her guests were men that needed a place to sleep, get up from and go to work. My mother did well as a landlady. Alf built himself another pigeon loft, this one at ground level in the yard. I was 7 years old and had no idea in what direction to head even if I could escape this dreary environment. There was no way out and no way back. I suppose we had become what people would call normal; I think, the truth be told, we had become poor.

My introduction to my second place of learning was not as pleasant or straightforward as my first enrolment in academia. Would it be an overstatement to say it was alarming and dramatic and every bit as terrifying as the black dungeon of a place misnamed our new home? The house had left me shellshocked. We now lived in a place called Catford; I recall it had SE6 after it. It cost one and halfpence for the bus ride to school. This amount is forever burned in my memory as I would in the not-too-distant future walk to and from my new school and save the threepence. The school stood behind a formidable and dreary structure, 'the Church'. Gargoyles peered down at any would-be assailant. The bus by some twist of fate stopped directly in front of the church. I had never been in a church before. I wish I could say it was as fascinating and as compelling as my first school experience, but it wasn't. The school and church were named after some obscure saint. The principal was a sombre person with dark brown nicotine-stained fingers; in a few brief seconds he struck terror into the heart of this 7-year-old. I sat and listened to the benefits of being a good Catholic boy and being allowed to attend such a school, so I had better be a good little boy. I was not sure if this was a warning of impending doom, a suggestion or advice, or the man with the puffy red face was willing to inflict much pain to make me a good little boy.

I was indeed, fortunate. I would be able to stay for school dinners (lunch) at the expense of the church. You see, I had been 'done'. Now there is full-immersion baptism and then there is the common baptism or christening that takes place at a very early age. There must be thousands if not millions of people out there who have been done and don't know about it. I recalled that Drip the Irishman with silver hair had been my father's foreman and close confidant; at times he was referred to as my godfather. A position only held by Catholics and the Mafia. There has to be a message in that somewhere. My parents must have been desperate for my mother to have handed me over to an ill-defined fate she as a child had lived through, but there I was: with my grandparents the O'Bryants, no less, the O now back to give us more of a Catholic sound, and better Catholics one would be hard-pressed to find. They being from Southern Ireland and all, it was like some secret code of entry. Mother was saying we all came from a good Catholic home and there were the bits of paper on the desk saying I had been done. So, done I must have been. So, I was in, free lunches and all.

How did I get from a pleasant, carefree world, having a little happy life, to this new life with such speed and finality? One day I was in one environment, and glad to be there, the next transported across some invisible timeline and thrust into a world of barrow boys and chimney sweeps. To live in an unpleasant and joyless house that appeared to be out of a Dickensian novel, a hostile and unfriendly place, all in less than twenty-four hours. In the London blitz, the Luftwaffe was dropping bombs all over the place. How on earth could they have possibly missed this bastion of British culture and learning? It was incomprehensible. Perhaps it was not worth the cost of a single German bomb, such a dismal and forlorn place it was.

There were no flowers or grass to be had anywhere, nothing but dirty, grimy, dark brown brickwork on the outside of the school and uninspiring institutional paintwork inside. The buildings encircled the playground. All that was missing were the guards and barbed wire. The playground surface was covered with a hard, gravel-like material called tarmac, a paving material made with crushed stone and tar mixed then heated together, a material suitable for building roads. If you fell or got pushed or knocked down, a recurring happening in my case, part of your outer extremities would get damaged and grazed: mild words to describe cuts, welts, lacerations and open wounds that would appear on the body when contacting said hard ground. It is an ideal material for making roads and runways but not for small bodies to bounce off.

What this wee Catholic lad did get for being from an out-of-date, lower-working-class home, was a small bottle of milk every day free, courtesy of the local London borough of Catford. Delivered in steel crates, milk monitors would, with all the air of authority that a 7- or 8-year-old could muster, place the bottle on the desk in front of us. It took only milliseconds for all the bottles to be sucked dry with slurping and panting, leaving only the air to be drawn up through the paper straw, until it collapsed and the bottle was empty. Indeed, we were a hungry, thirsty lot. Malnourished children surrounded me but this gift was to keep many a child from starvation. I believe it was so they, the elusive them or they, could build up our little bodies so should Her Majesty's Government need soldiers in the future, we would be able to answer the call.

We also had free lunch that was absolutely, utterly awful. We used to get fed, and I mean fed as in bovines. We sat at long tables, stretching from one end of a hall to the other, ending at the kitchen doors. Each row of tables was set about three feet apart. Down this aisle came two bent-double elderly women, each looking as if she was single-handedly responsible for all the world's problems and possibly the two world wars. This unhappy-looking couple would push a trolley between the rows of tables occupied by the smelliest, dirtiest children in all South London and maybe the north as well; all looked similar to my attackers from some years ago. I lived in fear that one of them might recognize me and try to finish the job. A self-inflicted paranoia. What child in this place would have the means to travel to where I had lived? Had it been within walking distance, I would have already left. I don't know. Was this divine retribution for having had six or seven years of a pleasant, enjoyable childhood? I was now made to sit next to what must have been the dirtiest of the dirty. Was it to instil in me a humble spirit to teach me a lesson? At an early age I had found the runny nose of Drip digging somewhat fascinating; to be surrounded by snotty-nosed kids at lunchtime did not constitute a pleasant dining environment. Once I asked to be moved, which became a humiliating and somewhat painful experience. I was dragged back and plonked heavily with a certain amount of Catholic vindictiveness between two smelly playmates. I thought it had been a reasonable request, the teachers not so much.

The portable table pushed with a great deal of panting and effort was transport for the large cooking pots of food that sat precariously on top. On the bottom tier of the trolley would be the refills. We must have been a hungry mob of the great unwashed: the containers were always empty by the end of lunchtime.

Prepositioned plates sat in front of the recipient, or victim, depending on one's palate. Whatever you do, do not move the dish from said position, neither left nor right. The food would be dumped on the plate by one of the two serving women, Happiness or Glum, who came along at the same speed every day. With a rhythmic flow, the ladle plunged into the depths of one of the vats. Out would come first a large dollop of mashed potatoes. Plop. Centre of the plate every time then an equally large dollop of cabbage or other nondescript veggie, and the outstanding culinary accomplishment the runny, watery ladle of mincemeat.

Should the plate be moved, the best one could expect would be, 'Sorry dear, but you did move the plate. Just put the plate on the edge of the table and scoop it in. It's all good food.' So, don't move the plate. Whatever they ladled out I could only ever manage to eat half of it. There was always someone who would take my plate and give me their empty one. No one was allowed to waste food. This sleight of hand worked well for me, as it did for the all-consuming monster on the other side of the table. Then I got the timing wrong. In front of me was my empty plate as Happiness and Glum were making their second pass. An empty plate signalled a hungry child whose dish was to be refilled once more to the brim. I had just got rid of most of my disgusting stuff, and now I had another lot that could not be eaten or disposed of. I was always a small child, but even I could not squish through the locked gates to escape this daily torment. I just sat there, tears streaming down my face; food was not to be wasted and punishment awaited such an ingrate as myself. I would never get this lot down. I made it to the boys' bogs followed by one of the teachers in hot pursuit. I closed the door before he could grab me, and then made foul noises.

'Boy, are you all right?' He never even knew my name.

'Food poisoning, sir,' I called out, sobbing, desperate not to be made to eat whatever it was, food being a kinder description. I had to get away. The words food poisoning were magic.

'Impossible,' I could almost hear him thinking. An efficient and practical approach from the voice on the other side of the door: 'All right, finish what you're doing, have a drink of water or something, then go outside and sit down.'

'Please sir, I am all right, sir. Just got to sit for a while, sir.'

Silence.

'Can I go home, sir?'

'No, you jolly well can't. Drink some water or something.' It was obvious this person had limited medical knowledge if drinking water was the primary medication for food poisoning. I heard footsteps receding outside.

I eventually found if I hid and did not line up to march into the hall, no one would miss me. I was just one amongst the many hungry dwarf-like minions. I discovered it was possible to go through the back door of the church proper and come out at the front and escape through the large medieval doors leading out on to the street, circumventing the locked gates. The church was empty apart for one or two wicked people, who were there every day in the same place. Other than the occasional sniffle or a cough as I passed them, I was invisible. They could, like the statues around the walls, be made of wood or plaster.

Providing I knelt, genuflected and observed the ritual, bob down, kneel, quick sign of the cross so as not to vaporize because of the disgusting sins that all 7-year-olds are guilty of, everything was okay. I had to be back before the lunch break was over; as long as I was in line when the bell went, no one would look for me. With hindsight, I think had I never turned up again, no one would have missed me, but I was never brave enough to try. I had three pennies bus fare that bought edible food and peace of mind as I sat on a bench out of sight. There is a lot to be said for English fish and chips wrapped in old newspaper. Not only had my location for learning changed, but the vernacular and lexicon had to change as well; if I was to survive, I should have to keep quiet, stay low, and sit at the back of the class and not be there.

One of the first things Alf – now renamed Dad, no longer Daddy – built when renovating was a bathroom, which did not solve the grimy kid problem in South London. It did, however, make our lives more comfortable, and we had a little more room once we got rid of the tin bathtub and the wall that separated the kitchen and scullery.

The children in my school spoke a different language to me. I had Father and Mother; they had the Old Man and Old Lady. I had 'Don't do that, please', they had 'Sod off' and worse. I found it was best to adopt this new language, as until I did, I was either the stupid boy at the back of the class that spoke posh, confronted with 'Err, what you doing eer anyway?' or I got bashed by someone bigger. Best, don't talk at all. A country divided by the lexicon. Thing, being pronounced fing with init at the end; replacing all and any kind of punctuation, it is a land of semantic gymnastics. England was and still is a strange land. It was the world that I had to adjust to and survive in at 7 years of age, and survive I did. There was never any poor little me; no one was interested. All the time I lived in that house and went to that school, I never made one friend.

When at school, I was not only dyslexic but also, I had what today is called sleep apnoea. Two conditions hardly known then if at all, but one that robbed me of sleep. I could scarcely keep my eyes open and did at times fall asleep at my desk only to be woken up by a thrown blackboard duster – a large, heavy wooden object used to clean the chalk off the blackboard or used by teachers as an object to throw at lazy little boys. The blackboard duster was a missile sent flying through the air to hit any person who was guilty of some infraction of a petty rule. If awake, it was large enough to see and avoid.

The deadliest and fastest object was the school chalk. This fast travelling projectile was small and easily handled by teachers, small and large, male and female. It could be hurled at high speed to connect my nodding head. I was not the only one to fall asleep. I was, however, noticed even over that vast expanse from the front of the class. I had made a tactical and strategic choice into what I thought was a safe area. Other children fell asleep or nodded off around me as well, but for different reasons; some due to a lack of nourishment, others because of broken homes or domestic violence that kept them awake through the night, as a mother and father did battle. Still others because of child abuse that was never far away or spoken of or even understood. I, along with other more fortunate children, had a father who did not drink and worked hard to feed his family. My lifestyle downgrade was the result of my father's bankruptcy through humping his attorney's wife, not a wise choice when in business.

It was cost-effective to send me to this school, and an easy way out that entailed a short bus ride, cost one and halfpence one-way. Once I was there, I think they just forgot where they had put me. Being the stupid boy at the back of the class helped a great deal. The strange thing is I never knew that we were part of the system I was now in; I had no idea that I was poor. My mother ran a boarding house, dad had work, and we always had food to eat. I never went to bed hungry, but many did.

It was at this not-so-early age I learned to read. I devoured books. Through some quirk of fate, a female teacher, who spoke a different kind of English to that which surrounded me, took an interest and gave her time to teach me how to read. I can honestly say that learning to read was the only skill I learned or was motivated to excel in by that one and only teacher in all the time I was at that school. However, even those lessons were to come to an ignoble end.

I can't even recall how it started other than to say one day I got the hardest whack across the head any 8-year-old ever got. It was an ear-ringing, head-spinning, teeth-rattling smack across the side of my head. For what? Don't know. Maybe he was having a bad day, perhaps because he could get away with it, or it made him feel good, whatever. My ear was blue. Mother, now Old Lady, had been brought up and taught in a convent school, so she knew all about the bitterness of heart and petty vindictiveness that many religions foment. When she saw my ear, she was down to that school like an air-to-ground missile. Catholic or no Catholic, no one was going to give one of her children a whack like that. No appointment: just on the bus, one and a halfpenny fare please, and down to the school. Wouldn't you know it the first teacher she came across was my pleasant reading teacher? My mother came from what one would call Irish peasant stock; born in England yes, but she had gallons of Irish blood pumping through her body and the Irish paddy that went with it.

The men could beat the living daylights out of one another, or their wife and kids or womenfolk when possessed by the demon drink, but woe betides anyone who would lift a non-Celtic hand to touch one of their own. It was like kicking the proverbial junkyard dog. Irene had years of anger and bitterness in her head and heart for religion and church. Nuns, priests and the Pope himself were all about to be impaled with her tongue. Unfortunately, my reading teacher was the first person Mother Dear met as she breached the outer gates and stormed in looking for a living target. I never had another reading lesson. Maybe she was just a relief teacher. I am sure she never got the sack as she had done nothing wrong. Perhaps she was just tired with all of us peasants in the South (pronounced Saff) of London, and the great unwashed.

Once I spoke the vernacular, I was left alone. Playground fights were plenty accompanied by the usual cries of 'Fight, fight!' and everyone would dash to see what was going on, maybe because there was so much abuse in many homes, or we all had a common enemy: the system. There was not too much bullying.

Most teachers I think did their best to instruct what must have been to them just an over-full class of misfits and dirty little people who did not want to be there. The teachers were mainly men, having returned from war, with many emotionally and some physically damaged. All with their nightmares and grief, but they tried.

In the schooling of that time, there was no such thing as sex education; we never needed it. There was always some slightly older boy who was able to enlighten us about what bits went where. Also, in the boys' bogs were misshapen, disfigured drawings etched on the walls and doors that portrayed the female form, along with phone numbers, made up or real, and what to expect if making a call. Poems and limericks, some rather amusing, showed a degree of literary potential. Of course, one would have to be a cryptographer to decipher the misspelled profanity, but they had a general idea. Then there was the dirty talk, or rude things said about Mary, Fatima, Bernadette and Joan, or some other poor innocent girl child. The names of female saints are pretty limited, so parents don't have a wide range to choose from when naming good little Catholic girls.

Mary or whoever, when walking home from school near a vacant bomb site had 'a man show her his willie' – 'No he never' – 'Did so' – 'What did it look like?' Mary or whoever was then a dirty little girl because some pervert had flashed her. Also, it would go around the school. Mary was a little tart, and in our evil infant minds, we thought of all kinds of childlike thoughts but had no real knowledge of what Mary had seen or done or not done. 'Naa, you ain't never seen a real willie' – 'Have so too' – 'Whose?' – 'Me uncle's, that lives with us, when me mum's out.'

Sometimes a boy would let everyone know 'the flasher's back' and the offending dirty old man would have to quicken his pace to get away from the rowdy kids yelling, ''Eer mister, show us ya willie, show ya, willie.' No one ever thought of telling the police or the old man or old lady; it was too much fun seeing him run, and it would bring too much trouble for us. It would be our fault because what were we doing there?

Then there was the adventurous little boy who dropped his pencil next to a desk so he can look up a girl's dress as he bent to retrieve said item from between her feet, all the boys then asking him what the colour of her knickers was, she defending her honour by saying he got the colour wrong. Not navy-blue ones like he just told everyone, followed by the inevitable chorus of 'Prove it, prove it, show us ya knickers then.' All this from prepubescent children with no lasting damage inflicted.

The damage would come when he or she would lie still at night, dreading the footsteps, listening if he would pass by or stop at the door. The turning of the doorknob, the groping hands, then only being able to sleep a few short hours or dreading to sleep as that's when things happened. If you stayed awake, you could say, 'I'll tell me mum.' Knowing full well you never would, and he knew it too. Who would believe you? Then a short restless sleep, and then the inevitable blackboard duster or chalk thrown at your nodding head the next day at school. At school everyone could make dirty jokes and laugh at the silly old sods or nasty old buggers, but at night it was different.

Alternatively, the little girl sitting next to you in class asks, 'Does your dad touch you?' You don't know what she means and even if you did, what could an 8-year-old do? It was best to keep quiet. Who would believe your uncle would do such a thing to you when Mum was out shopping or working late.

Best keep quiet and take the sixpence he gave you the next day for 'our little secret'. A tanner got you into Saturday morning pictures; why you might even get a shilling if he was drunk. That would get you into the Saturday morning pictures and sweets or ice cream, or you could also take a friend with you.

In three short years that felt like a lifetime, I learned a lot, maybe too much. I discovered that all coppers are bent. Prisons are full of innocent people, frequently family, fathers or uncles, as the police are always 'picking on 'em, ain't they'. This was revealed to me by the bigger kids at school. The age difference between an 8-year-old and an 11-year-old is enormous when it comes to emotional issues; I was to find out a larger boy can seriously do damage to a smaller 8-year-old boy.

A teenager called Derek Bentley shot and killed a policeman. Shock and outrage throughout the land. The papers were all of the same opinion and they made sure the public could not help but know about it. One does not shoot our unarmed bobbies and get away with it, this is not America, and similar comments. Editorials in the UK would formulate an opinion. As an 8-year-old who had only just started to read, I did not have an opinion, but for a one-and-a halfpence bus ride, I could take you to a place where everyone had one. 'He was being stitched up by the police, as they always do it' or 'Weren't his fault, were it, and 'e never done nuffing'. Whereas my mother's attitude was 'Let the little bugger swing' and other comments such as 'If you don't sort yourself out, that's how you're going to end up.' Why my mother thought I, as an 8-year-old, was going to shoot police officers I have no idea.

From an early age, it was established 'I was not going to amount to much'. I remember Bentley as he had the same name as a very upmarket vehicle. The shooting took place in the London borough of Croydon. For me, this could have been in Timbuktu, but geographically it was only a nine- or ten-minute bus ride away. For the total cost two and halfpence, or seven miles from the school. Most of the older kids knew someone that knew someone else. Or a father, brother or distant relative. Who in turn knew Derrick Bentley; so they said. In the telling, the stories got bolder and the storyteller more important as he knew a real criminal who had been 'banged up for doing a copper'.

Alternatively, he was close to someone who knew for sure he was being stitched up as 'Derrick was a real gem'. I learned that Mother's opinion did not count for a great deal when it came to playground politics after being bounced or bumped (a method of inflicting discomfort on a boy by holding legs and arms, then raising and lowering said boy to slam on the ground; unpleasant in the extreme, when done on a durable tarmac playground.)

I learned whatever you heard you kept to yourself as a week or two later a bigger boy would come and bash you for starting rumours and lies about his family, sister or brother. I learned for one and a halfpenny bus ride, one could get two sides of a story both different but equally as important and believable, subject to that short bus ride across the divide.

I learned that uncles and boyfriends of the older boys' sisters could find stuff that fell off the back of a truck, and it usually was good stuff as well. They just happened to be walking past. That the ladies that my mum called tarts, were nice to me when I asked, 'What's that little chain around your ankle for?' and they would say, 'Come back when you're bigger and I'll show you.' Alternatively, 'You're going to be a little heartbreaker, ain't ya.' They were nice. I think they liked me. If they were with a bloke, they would sometimes say to the bloke, 'Go on, give 'im sumfing.' However, I never told my mum I used to talk to them.

I learned that if you spoke posh, you often got bashed by someone; so, don't talk posh. That if you hung around Catford dog stadium and said: 'Look after your car, mister?' If the mister had a good night at the dogs and won money, you would get something, or get nothing if he had lost. (How on earth an 8-year-old could look after a vehicle defies logic.)

Even then, things were changing. Nothing dramatic as when we first became poor, but a change was in the air. Just a short time before we left for greener pastures, a woman called Ruth Ellis was hanged for the murder of a 'nasty bit of work', my mother's words, not mine. Again, I had no opinion, and no one at school was passionate about her; a shame as she looked like one of the ladies with an ankle chain. I'm sure she was a nice person. My mother did say 'It's a travesty.' I asked her what she meant. Being told she should never have been hanged, this seemed strange to me.

A young man, who did not shoot a policeman, was hanged in the place of his friend who did the shooting; a pretty woman whose photo I liked killed someone. My mother expressed strong feelings that she should not have been hanged, calling her 'a poor little cow'. My mother would see others as livestock from time to time. A Right Cow would mean Very Bad. She can be a Real Cow that one, not too bad sometimes, and a Poor Little Cow, compassion or sadness for the said cow. When I saw her photo, I thought she looked lovely, and also formed an opinion. All these are merely memory milestones.

Sometime while at this school, rationing in the UK stopped altogether – the world was getting back to normal. I was to meet and work with an older man, a German immigrant in Australia, who told me that he was a POW from the Russian Front and was only released in 1952, seven years after the war came to an end. Another friend who grew up in postwar Europe told me they still had to buy antibiotics and medicine on the black market until the mid-1950s, a decade after the end of the war. Britain started to come out of it earlier, but then we had won, hadn't we? No more free school dinners. Only the desperately poor had free lunches now. We now had to pay. Every Monday, you had two shillings or half a crown for a week's school dinners. That meant I was now making the princely sum of about three and a half bob if you included my bus fare at threepence a day.

I remember no matter where we went or what we did as a family, somehow everyone would end up fighting about something. I think my parents just got used to each other or had what one would call mutual dependency.

I recall I played only one game of football and one game of cricket, both unsuccessfully. I managed to get the ball once after standing around on a cold, wet day in the mud for what I thought was forever; I ran it to the goalmouth. I was just about to put it through the posts when someone took the ball away from me, so I spent the rest of the match once more standing around in the wet and the cold, thinking at a tender age that this was a waste of bloody time. The game of cricket was much the same. I stood for an age, miles away on the other side of the park out of sight, a distant place that in cricket is given some strange name. Then I got to have my turn with the bat. I gave the ball one hell of a whack, and it looked as if it would go forever. Some dimwit standing almost outside of the park caught it. One boy grabbed the bat out of my hands, and an argument ensued.

'I hit the ball. Why do I have to give you the bat?'

'You were caught out.'

'But I hit the ball. No one told me anything about out. I want another go!' Then being sent right out near the other side of the park, again a place where I spent the rest of the game standing around, with a young mind thinking this is a total waste my bloody time.

Alf the builder was the one-time rear-gunner Titch Brown. I believe the smaller they were, the easier to fit into the turret, Titch/Alf had flown with men called Rhodesians. From a country somewhere called by that name – Rhodesia. My parents went into the city of London proper and got all kinds of stuff to tell people what and where Rhodesia was. The world, in general, had suffered a lot of damage and millions killed in the Second World War. The British colonies, as they were then, had to restock. They needed people to rebuild, and pay taxes to keep politicians in a lifestyle they didn't deserve; and if the people who answered the call had children, all the better as they might be needed in the future to send off to war. It's always good to plan. Rhodesia had lost so many men. Rhodesia needed restocking. The brochures were all sunshine and marshmallows.

This all took place before the end of the school term. I told them I would not be back as I was off to Africa. It made me quite the celebrity. No one from my school had ever travelled more than five miles from home. Then the school holidays ended. I should have gone back to school. The problem was I had told everyone I was off to Africa. I thought it best not to go back. Two weeks later, there was a knock at the door: it was the School Board Man. His job is to find out why the drones where not in class being indoctrinated. A few short weeks after that encounter with the school board, the five of us were walking down the road, each with a suitcase and Sharon wheeling her favourite doll's pram, off to catch the boat train to Southampton. I got away just in time.

Chapter 2

To Rhodesia and Back

The trees at night ask,
'If they have no roots, how do they survive?'

Old Russian proverb

When I say we walked to catch the boat train each with one suitcase, it sounds as if we were a family of Polish refugees making our way from East to West. Nothing would be further from the truth. Emigrants leaving the UK saw themselves as escaping to a new and better life. This escape did not involve crawling across open ground and avoiding mines, gun towers, lights and dogs. No! Exit from the United Kingdom was an orderly one, the hardships incurred if any would be eating British Railway sandwiches, or walking in the rain to the train station if it had indeed been raining. The walking distance from our front door to the station was too close to warrant a bus ride. As for the sandwiches one had a choice, whereas with the weather – not so. You could say at the start of our adventure the weather was cold brisk and dry, with a sunny afternoon later. The sandwiches made by British Rail – the less said, the better.

The waiting before we left became unbearable, not the unbearable when you are waiting for Christmas or even a birthday. The unbearable was every knock on the front door, expecting the School Board Man outside, ready to drag yours truly back to Stalag 17, the name now given to my school; the older boys had renamed Saint Whatshisname after seeing a war movie about escaping prisoners of war in the Second World War. I had now missed several weeks of schooling; this did not worry my parents over much, and it gave me no concern whatever as no one would tearfully say, 'I'll miss you, Robert' as I left. Mum's lodgers, on the other hand, would miss her, as Mum's house had become their home. That was because she ran a tight, clean ship that had regular feeding times with wholesome food and plenty of it.

We sold all the furniture with the house. Alf had done a magic job of renovation. The son of a canny Scot who had in earlier years owned a horse and cart, and not forgetting the dogs. A wee Jock whose saying always was 'Where there's muck there's money' (muck pronounced mock), he had indeed made money out of other people's old junk. Coming from such a background, you can bet your life my parents would have turned a healthy little profit on the small, dirty, little dwelling I had first entered. I am sure mother had a teapot somewhere, the same as many women in working-class Britain, a nest egg full of crinkled banknotes amassed from the boarding house. Irene was an excellent landlady.

I recall one of the boarders did not believe we were going. He made no effort to find new digs and no arrangements to move. Come the last few days and my mother was running up the road to a colleague – is colleague the correct word for landladies in South London who ran boarding houses? – to find him a place. I think she was good at what she did. She had some strict house rules, one of them being 'If you throw up you clean up'. Many, including me, saw her as hard and more than a little argumentative and abrasive, which she was. That said, I couldn't remember any of them wanting to leave her place once they had secured a bed in the house. She never had a massive turnover of lodgers; it became home. None wanted her to close down or move. Much to the horror of our neighbours, Mother Dear sold the house to a black man from Nigeria. Drapes, carpets, everything other than household pots and pans.

Then one day we took the casual walk to the station on the first leg of my life-changing journey much like the Polish refugees that we were not. The first train took us into London proper, to catch no ordinary train, but the boat train. Our carriage door would open and an adult would peer in, see our compartment was full of children and a family and move on, saying, 'That one's occupied.' The more abrasive: 'That's got kids in' as if we were contagious.

The conductor was walking along the platform, closing doors or telling people to close the doors, then helping some latecomer get into a carriage by shoving his or her case behind them. Well-wishers and family members who would not be travelling, rushing to get onto the platform before the train left. Doors slamming with that muffled definitive kind of *clunk*, a sound that only doors of a departing train can make; then the sudden *bump* before the train moved, first moving us back just a foot or two as the engine coupled, but even that was movement, proving something was happening. The loud hissing of steam as the engine slowly started to move. The last hurried slamming of doors, hands and arms trying to hang on but knowing the bond will be, has to be, broken. The massive locomotive wheels spinning, trying to get traction. Metal against metal then the slow crawl becoming a walking pace, then a gentle run, too fast for anyone to stay with. We were on our way. At last, thank you, British Rail, and about time.

Waiting to board the ship, in the departure lounge, everyone was dead quiet at first, a bit like the church that I used to sneak through. Some shoulder to shoulder, but no one talking to one another outside of his or her little circle. Then, as they stake their claim to a particular table, bench or bar, they become more confident, you hearing the lighthearted banter and the severe but light-hearted rebuke. The do's and don'ts about life in Africa, from friends and family, who probably had not ever set foot out of England. The weird jokes that adults tell one another, 'When you come back to see us, we don't want you bringing back an African princess with a bone in her nose and piccaninnies in tow.' Advice from an old African hand, what was a piccaninny? Mothers to daughters: 'Darling, please don't brush along the walls; you're going to get that nice new dress dirty before we even go anywhere.' Fleeting memories of a red-headed boy with holes in his sweater, telling me not to get dirty.

We crossed over a bridge leading from the waiting lounge. Through a big double door on the side of the ship proper, then I was on board. One second, on land and a few steps later at sea. You would never have known – there was no movement at all. Strange, I thought we would all go up one of those ladders that hang from the side that you see in the movies. The ship was the *Edinburgh Castle* and it looked enormous. There was the most exhilarating labyrinth of passageways and stairs that went from deck to deck, waiting to be discovered. The stairs were impressive; they would make for an entertaining climb in rough weather. They were incredibly steep. Everywhere was painted white, bulkhead walls, ceilings, everywhere other than the floor that was polished so you could see a reflection. Handrails ran along the clean white walls, each anchored to the innards of the ship by sizeable, robust brass fixtures, handrails and balustrades similar to those in big houses. We as a family all went up on deck to the lounge. It was getting close to the magical hour called departure time. Some people were now excited, others not so much at the prospect of the goodbyes, walking their visitors to the exit. 'I'll write, promise', 'Love you, miss you' already a lie or a mystery to a 9-year-old, as we had not even pulled away from the quay yet. The ship's horn blew, a deep echoing sound one never forgets, to tell the visitors it was time to leave the boat. The lengthy and stressful episode for passengers getting on board a vessel became as lengthy and stressful for visitors getting off. Reluctant people, mostly visitors, moving out onto the deck, some looking none too happy, wanting to get this beastly exercise of goodbyes over with as soon as possible. Passengers crowded against the railings of the ship; I pushed through the crowd to see what was happening. Then the long, continual final blast of the ship's horn.

Members of the crew walked around, advising: 'Please move to the gangways, and make your way off the boat' – choreographed mundane rituals of each voyage. The crowd thinned until only the passengers were left on board, looking across the void that separated passengers from visitors.

Comfortable old places, homes and familiar streets, pubs, clubs along with family and friends, all traded now for adventure and a new world that all hoped would be better. I hung over the side, looking down, thinking the ship was enormous; I could see men running back and forth, lifting ropes as thick as a man's arm or leg and dropping them over the side of the quay into the water. Then the streamers were thrown – all different colours, hundreds of thin brightly coloured paper strings yards if not miles long – trying to keep connected for as long as possible, the last thin thread to what is now past. People were shouting at who knows who, family members, old friends. Some wag in the crowd yelled out, 'What about that ten bob you still owe me? Pay up before you leave.' Humour that only the British know how to use when sad, unsure or fearful. No one knew who this was aimed at, as a nervous ripple of laughter flowed over the crowd. A group of people started to sing a wartime song, the words soon lost on the sea breeze coming in across the harbour. Small groups of people stood on the quayside for a long time, wondering. It was precisely 2 o'clock on a Thursday afternoon as the Union–Castle mail steamship slipped her moorings.

As a 9-year-old boy hanging over the side, wondering whether this was actually happening and thinking I could not be so lucky; had the trip been cancelled or my parents had changed their minds? The thought of going back to Stalag 17 was a nightmare. Just how jammy could one 9-year-old get? I learned that goodbyes for adults were exhausting, whereas with children, it just meant going someplace else.

The further we pulled away from England's shores, the more people settled down. Later I fell asleep to a new sound, the soft *thud-*

thud of the ship's engines somewhere deep down in the belly of my new home. No one fell overboard.

People were on deck early that day we were to arrive in Cape Town, looking out to sea trying to be the first to sight land, eyes screwed up almost closed as if to gain extra range to one's vision. Our new home in the distance was unidentifiable. Landing at Cape Town, the passengers were a diverse lot. South Africans, returning home after a trip; English, Europeans, starting a new life at the foot of Africa. Small groups, handfuls going here or there across Africa, Southern Rhodesia, Northern Rhodesia, names of new places soon to be called home. A few would travel by ship on to Dar es Salaam in Tanganyika and others to Mombasa in Kenya. Africa had so many strange, exotically named places. I was desperate to see Table Mountain, overlooking Cape Town. Passports, luggage keys, tickets, did we need money? Should we buy South African cash? We would travel first to Johannesburg by train; being a sleeper carriage, we would go through the night, arriving the next day. The heat told us we were in another country; it was hot in Africa. We had someone loading our bags onto a trolley. A porter pushed the cart loaded with luggage. A rather large man who spoke strange English came to our carriage to ask my father if he would look after his daughter, as she was travelling alone in the next carriage. I had never heard of someone being afraid of travelling alone on a bus or a train before. One could say travel in England in the 1950s was safe. Maybe the nation was exhausted from the war to be anything other than pleasant to one another. Five years of bloody conflict was enough fighting for anyone; they had to stop to catch their breath. It was the first time I saw a grown-up wearing short trousers other than on the beach. The trip at best could be termed mundane or was I expecting too much having just arrived in Africa? A steward walked the train with a miniature xylophone, announcing mealtimes. I explored the carriage and its fold-down beds, then walked to the dining car then the toilets. All very similar to British Rail apart from the fold-down bunks. Introduction to African travel was a letdown.

The journey ended at Johannesburg's Park Station. We stepped out onto a shaded part of the platform, in a tunnel of darkness, the panting porter bent over, starting to sweat in the heat of the day. He was white. Keeping out of the direct rays of the sun, we walked behind him, much like a funeral procession, and made our way to another platform, into bright African sunshine. Everyone was melting in the heat. There was still no sign of wild animals. I then saw the train that would carry us to the capital of Southern Rhodesia, Salisbury. My first glimpse of a real African train was a memorable sight; the train was straight off the silver screen, a cowboy train, an anachronistic steam locomotive with an item on the front that I thought was for pushing boulders and dead Red Indians off the tracks. The livery was dark brown and light beige, constructed of varnished wood panelling, Along the top in large letters was S.R.R for Southern Rhodesian Railways with each carriage numbered in the same colour paint. One carriage displayed the words DINING CAR, all the lettering being in gold. The contrast of gold lettering on the dark brown looked impressive even to a small boy. The carriages had little verandas at either end, so you could stand outside and watch the countryside going by. Steps up to the train were from ground level; unlike regular trains this one you boarded from the ground, not off a platform. Entering the coach proper, you made your way to your private saloon or berth by walking along the passage that ran down the length of one side of the carriage.

The further we travelled north, the more it became the Africa that I had imagined. In retrospect, one could say South Africa was not Africa. It is bits of Europe built right at the bottom of this vast expanse called Africa. Africa proper starts north of the Limpopo River or if you journey east or west outside the borders of South Africa itself. We spent three days on that train. Towards evening stewards came to make up our beds in the sleeper. At certain times someone with the miniature xylophone walked down the passageway to let passengers know it was mealtime. You could set a watch by this. When the track did a long slow right turn, you were able to sit in the carriage, looking out the window and see the locomotive pulling us at the front of the train, hot ash spewing out from the steam engine itself, as the stoker kept feeding the fire with coal for the boilers. Smoke belched out, black from the chimney of the locomotive, wafting along the top of the coaches. A light powdery soot was everywhere. The only way to overcome this was to keep the windows closed. Even then, this fine black powder found its way into everything, depositing a thin coating of black dust. Bathing was impossible; washbasins in the carriages where so small and meant just for hands and face. It was a painstaking exercise to uphold the appearance of civilization and cleanliness. However, this we did, as we are civilized.

Train travel over time is like sea travel; your body adjusts to the rhythmic movement of the swaying coaches much like the rolling and pitching and *thud-thud* of engines on a ship. Trains have the constant *clucky-de-cluck* of the wheels on steel tracks that after a time go unnoticed or have a hypnotic effect.

Sunsets and sunrises in Africa can be dramatic and awe-inspiring when seen for the first time. The intensity of colours viewed through the shimmering African heat rising off the veldt is vivid. The sun becomes blood red as it sinks slowly at the end of the day. It paints the African bush in different, unimaginable and indescribable shades and hues. Forms take on terrifying and exciting images. Hostile silhouettes lurk under or behind every bush and tree as we flash past. Are there animals that can run this fast? Maybe a cheetah or another big cat might leap up and grab a small boy off his perch. Snakes might slither onto the train when we stopped at a siding. Threats produced by an ignorant, tired mind, I started to think about going inside to the safety and security of the carriage lights. Each evening this perfect performance was repeated by the sinking sun. I was held captive; Africa looked so big. The day ended, Earth agreed with a slight drop in temperature that would make sleep almost bearable, the rhythmic *clickety-clack* of steel wheels on rail becoming a lullaby as I slept through the night helped by the soothing sounds of the train.

African mornings are more commanding and aggressive than sunsets; looking out over this land, someone once said with a great deal of irony in her voice, 'Another perfect "bloody" day in Africa.' When the sun gracefully goes down, it gives no idea that it will re-emerge with such a vengeance. What starts as a bright, pleasant early morning becomes a scorching, unforgiving mass of heat. The day starts with cool and agreeable temperatures which rise to incredible highs, sucking the life out of you. The unceasing heat, hour after hour, day after day can become unbearable, rushing wind as the train chugged forward was warm, giving no relief to the passengers. If it was not a new adventure, it could have become tedious. The African sun hangs in the clear, azure sky. Fierce, aggressive, consuming, it seems far away and small, unlike the innocuous setting sun that brings the cool at the close of day. You cannot look directly at the rising sun; its blinding light giving off glass-like shards that cut into one's eyes, making them water or producing dancing dots. It's impossible to gaze at anything for any length of time without squinting or shielding one's eyes from the penetrating glare. The sun dominates life as it marks the start of another earth-scorching day. The countryside, a quaint European expression, is a term totally inadequate to describe the harsh, arid veldt. We sped north through mopane scrubland and then acacia trees, short and stumpy. Everything was crooked and misshapen, the only straight timber being the telegraph poles that ran the length of the rail lines. The misshapen flora surrendered to the desert of Bechuanaland. Not many trees here, the veldt took on a new appearance as the topography changed, and we skirted the Kalahari Desert. Heat thermals came off the scorched African earth, even at an early hour, hindering vision. The same sun that heralded the end of the day was back with a vengeance, hanging in the sky white hot and life-draining, the exquisiteness of it all now gone.

Every so often we pulled in to a siding and stopped. We were on a single line, and unlike England where two opposing passenger trains flash past, giving impressions of incredible speed, here we had the lazy *chuff-chuff* of the steam engine and the hissing of escaping energy with the engineer opening and closing valves in preparation for the wait. Our massive conglomeration of steel, steam and water called the locomotive slowed then stopped. It settled for the long delay, waiting for its oncoming clone from the opposite direction. It was surrounded by dozens of black people. They look withered and almost lifeless. With parched skin, stretching out hands, dry, empty palms begging for money or whatever. Dark skin wrinkled and creased from the sun and the barren, harsh world they survived in – no excitement here of the Hollywood screen. No Tarzan and Jane or happy chimp, just the never-ending scramble and begging to be given something, anything; to survive another day.

This Africa was then and still is today at times a wretched place to live. The African salute greets everyone from the civilized world. Surrounding, crushing crowds, sometimes small but most times large in numbers. If not begging, then trying to sell wood or stone carvings that when placed on an even level surface stand lopsided. People still buy them even if they have no place for them to stand; they will send them home as gifts for Christmas. Black Africa is always asking, asking, asking. I was not aware of it; I was seeing the inevitable result of tribalism, witchcraft and a slower work ethic to be followed later by *Uhuru*, freedom. I stepped down with my father from our old-world carriage with the verandas at each end, onto Africa's parched earth. We stood in the dust and heat, no concrete platform to alight on here or orderly footpath to stretch one's legs with a well-mannered gentlemanly stroll. Passengers were stepping down and looking around and wondering should the train move, would we have time to get back on?

My father was talking to a gentleman with an enormous handlebar moustache; he was ex-Royal Air Force, a Rhodesian. An old African hand. Alf, my father, was also in the RAF, Bomber Command.

The gentleman with a red nose and big moustache was in Fighter Command. A real Spitfire pilot I heard as I stood impatiently next to my father. Strangely, five years of bloody conflict and death were often relived and regurgitated; people would probably do so for the next ten or fifteen years. Their war and memories were as fresh as yesterday. A time I knew little or nothing about, it was how my mother got us into a street party at the coronation of Queen Elizabeth. Mother had been through the London Blitz, heard the Doodlebugs and all; so for a day, she became 'one of us, dear' and got me into a street party. My father and the 'chap', a term he used a lot along with jolly good show and tickety-boo, kept on talking. They had found common ground and I no longer existed. The big red nose used words like splendid and jolly good show often. At my school in South London, I knew nothing of Spitfires until informed by playground historians who would argue as to what was best: the Spitfire or the Hurricane. The Spit or the Hurry.

I had learned that Spitfire pilots and Hurricane pilots did exist but were like gods and never seen by the likes of myself or any other boy at school. Even when the boys did lie and say they knew one, we knew they were lying, and they never got away with it. One of the bigger boys would front them; it was heresy to take a fighter pilot's name in vain – he was one of 'The Few', in Churchillian prose. Now here was one talking to my father as if they were long-lost friends; I was awestruck and dared not pull my father away. Then the warrior god looked down at me and said: 'You're going to enjoy Rhodesia, young man, what do you say to that?' I look around at the teeming black hordes and blurted out, 'Sir, what do these people do in this place?' The Spit pilot laughed, not at me or the question. He grinned from under that great big moustache. 'Yes, quite! What exactly do they do?' It was not an answer to my question.

Others were foregoing the safety of their carriages. The big waxed moustache and Father parted company as we moved slowly away from the steps that would lead us back to the security of the train.

First a yard, gaining confidence as we walked to the front, kicking up dust that soon covered our shoes, outside the carriages to the steam engine. I saw a path from the railway line leading to some huts. The dwellings were of mud with no windows and just a door; it must have been dark inside. Nothing was straight; even the grass roofs could not be confused for thatching as in Europe. It was dry grass plonked on top of a mishmash of twisted and misaligned poles and mud. There is nothing elegant about African grass huts. Every square inch of the surrounds was unkempt. There was no uniformity in any of the buildings, the doors hanging in a lopsided, drunken manner with strips of old rubber as hinges, possibly cut from disused car tyres. Doors held closed by rusty wire, or some string wound around nails or pushed through a hasp. There was a fence with more crooked posts. The holes had not been dug deep enough, so the posts leaned at odd, veering angles held up mostly by even more rusty wire. The ground around the huts had been swept clean to the point of being sterile. The hot, unrelenting sun reflected off the polished surface. Rubbish was left in heaps only yards from the cleared circumference around each hut. Dogs, skinny and starving, nosed through the mounds of garbage, the heaps looking like inadequate walls of an enclosure or fort. There were no shiny, glistening black bodies of six-foot African warriors that escorted Tarzan. No animal skins or bright-coloured blankets or long, flowing headdresses. The myth of the Noble Savage dispelled. Yes, indeed, what do they do?

Soon after one starts a trip across Africa, you find the real Africa is a pathetic, squalid place. Populated by half-starving refugees, fleeing from one tribal conflict after another, political chiefs wallowing in bathtubs adorned with gold taps, bank accounts in Switzerland, along with a stable of high-end luxury vehicles and private jets. Africa is not for the faint-hearted. The world outside of Africa has a false impression. They think the black man is a smiling, jolly fellow sitting in the sun. With bright shiny teeth, with an ever-present smile, dark chocolate-brown pupils in a white surround of laughing eyes, eating watermelons. When in fact, there are few healthy teeth and the teeth one sees in a smile are discoloured, misshaped and poorly kept. Likewise, the Hollywood chocolate-brown eyes are mostly suffering from conjunctivitis; in Africa it is called the pink eye. Cataracts and glaucoma inflicted by the relentless African sun. TV and Hollywood have much to answer for: there is no Jungle Jim with starched razor-sharp creases in his trousers and no happy, yodelling muscle man swinging through the treetops. In the real Africa, I saw only wretched poverty and hardship. I even took pity on the dogs with their ribs protruding; I thought of old Joe's dogs, which he loved more than his thirteen children.

The down train passed and we continued our journey, leaving behind the small group of wretched humanity.

As we travelled north, I was allowed to spend as much time as I liked, other than mealtimes and bedtime, on the carriage veranda. My parents had now considered that I would not fall off if left alone. The natives were friendly, and even if not, they would have been unable to board a fast-moving train, other than the fact this was a somewhat slow train from time to time. I was left alone wondering about this Africa I found myself in. Africa, to me, was an incredible place. I had never seen such vast open spaces, yet the poverty, even to my young mind, was incomprehensible. I was at this early age getting an introduction to the real Africa.

There was no racism in my mind or my heart. I had endured three years in a school where I had to sit and eat with children whose hygiene was almost non-existent. Questionable social skills and no table manners, to say the least; here it was even worse. At most of the sidings, all I saw were snot-nosed blacks with poor eyesight dressed in rags and a woman with an over-aged infant sucking on a shrivelled breast, draining the last drop of nourishment from her, with the persistent buzzing and swarms of ever-present flies which never left their faces. I had never seen a female breast, only poorly defined drawings on the toilet door at school. Neither what I was looking at nor the crude drawings on the doors did justice to the female form.

My father was from a family of thirteen children. He had walked to school with no shoes; not kicking up the warm earth of some African village but through the biting cold of Derbyshire's sleet and snow in winter. My mother had been beaten and bashed by a drunken Irishman, and nuns. My parents understood life's hardships; they entered Africa with no racist convictions at all. Likewise, I did not view Africa through the eyes of race or a white man's understanding, but through the eyes and mind of a boy on his first real adventure. My questions had been simple, and mostly in regards to critical issues in my young life. These questions revolved around school. I asked whether I would go to a school with other white children; my concern was not a black-white issue: it was whether they would beat me up for talking differently. They all spoke English, I was told. Would they smell and have runny noses? No, they would not. It was a great comfort to me to know I would not be going to school with the children of the Les Miserables of Bechuanaland.

Africa, Africa, what a tragedy that truth is left untold. A boy learns of your raw savagery that replaces a dream. Reality is vicious with revelation. I wasn't disappointed or anything. My question to my parents after seeing the wizened blacks and filthy surroundings was: 'Why doesn't anyone help them?' My question nowadays would be why we still had to help them, with no tangible results after so long. They have stagnated for the past sixty years.

Rhodesia was a beautiful country for any young (white) boy to grown up in; it also had a very high quality of education. Within a short space of time, my parents found a small house in the suburbs, not that far from Cranborne. Cranborne was an old air force training facility; most of the streets had names of some relevance to the Second World War such as Alamein, Tobruk, and others. I think we lived on a road called Benghazi Drive. Rhodesia produced some excellent pilots who fought for King and Country, and per ratio, more born Rhodesians died for Britain than any other country in the Commonwealth. Too bad the effort put in by them was not reciprocated two decades later.

Once my parents had found their feet, having found work and a regular income, they looked for a more agreeable house, something better. Obviously when emigrating, this was the general idea – a better life; they found a large home on the southern side of Salisbury in a suburb called Waterfalls. It was somewhat rural. The house sat on a considerable acreage, with a deep well, that snakes from time to time slithered into. Until told otherwise and how dangerous it was, Keith and I would try and fish them out with the bucket.

A long dirt driveway stretched from the distant gate coming to a stop in front of the veranda. The house was fenced and gated all around with a three-foot diamond-mesh fence. It also had a resident dog, a very large Rhodesian ridgeback called George who came with the property. George did not like kaffirs, as blacks were derogatively known. He was wont to demonstrate this dislike from time to time; if he got out past the gate or was already out, George was not a very politically correct canine. The road leading to our new house was dirt as were most roads in the area in those days. It stretched from a tarred road that was the main road into Salisbury. I moved schools to Frank Johnston Primary. I don't recall the names of the teachers. I do remember the headmaster. He had been in the army in the last war as a Don R (motorbike dispatch rider). He invented a game called bicycle polo and had schoolboys riding around on their bikes whacking a ball with a hockey stick. All jolly good clean fun, as were most things in postwar Southern Rhodesia.

Life in Rhodesia was pleasant; yes, my mother had to work, but from a young boy's point of view, I found Rhodesia an incredible place to grow up. My father bought a car, a Chevrolet, a sizeable American vehicle. We travelled the country doing much sightseeing. A couple of times we went to Mozambique at Christmas, down to Beira, a coastal resort. My father borrowed one of those big army tents, the kind with the big poles at each end and a flysheet, real out-of-Africa stuff. We put a roof rack on the Chevy and off we went. We used to travel down in convoy with one or two friends as most places were very remote. The roads down to Mozambique were strip roads until we went through the border post at Umtali then they became dirt. I was travelling through a country I would spend many days fighting in, and one that would claim the lives of many young Rhodesians, more than a few being close friends. What was a strip road? It was two strips of tar laid down on a dirt road, each strip wide enough for the wheels on the left and the right of the vehicle to run, each strip being about a foot wide and some distance apart, running parallel to one another, as railway lines run. It was sufficient until you had a car coming towards you from the other direction. Then you had to move over so only the right-hand-side wheels were on the tar and the left side of the vehicle was on the dirt. When the cars had passed one another, dust was everywhere as the ground was scorched and dusty until the rains came. The sand was so thick that you had to drive with care before getting all four wheels back on the tar; one never knew if there was another vehicle approaching head-on, with billows of thick dust thrown up by the first vehicle making it impossible to see. What a beautiful country Rhodesia was. As I have already remarked, what a privilege to have spent time growing up there. Highlights of my young life in Rhodesia were many; getting a bike is just one of them. I was able to ride for miles.

Keith and I cycled to Mermaid's Pool, a family picnic place, a short drive from the city of Salisbury, to a swimming hole that had a fantastic waterfall that washed over the rocks. We use to slide down on inflated vehicle inner tubes – I would do a search and destroy operation in this area some fifteen years later in the bush war. We went camping with blankets and stuff tied on the crossbars of our bikes. We never knew or heard of a sleeping bag; even cooking utensils were rejects from Mother's kitchen. I cycled a couple of times with a school friend out to his family farm. Hot, dusty roads where the sand was so soft I had to push my bicycle, not being able to ride through it. I travelled that same road in the war years when on leave from the SAS to go hunting on that farm which stood empty with bullet holes in every window.

Sprawling Rhodesian farmhouses with broad verandas that ran all the way around, and vast open bush. So many memorable firsts, a schoolboy's dream come true. I was allowed to have my first real knife that I could wear on my belt and later a Daisy air rifle. I was infected and seduced by Africa; I was in love. After being in Rhodesia for a year, my parents had a new house built. I never had to change schools as I had my transport and cycled to school. I had my only dangerous snake incident that almost ended in tragedy at the new house. The garden was not much to look at, so my father had a three-ton truck of topsoil brought in. A high mound of soft, fresh dirt almost as big as the heaps of building sand I used to play in, and that is just what Sharon was doing. Playing. When I next looked, there it was just behind her, a somewhat agitated snake. In answer to what kind it was, it was a big mean angry one. I grabbed Sharon by the right arm, dragging her behind me; I think one could say there was a bit of uproar: all my parents could see was me pulling my sister around an unmade garden like a sack of Irish spuds. Give a dog a bad name! They thought I was doing this with malicious intent. Until they saw this monster, swaying two foot up off the ground ready to strike – it must have been a cobra – at the first person to approach it. Garden spades are an ideal anti-snake weapon when thrown on target. Everything in Africa survives by killing something else.

My mother's attitude started to change somewhat in the new house, and she seemed less happy if indeed she ever was. I kept hearing 'This can't go on' and slowly I heard about problems that never affected me, but indeed were starting to worry some adults. They use to stand around talking about the future, whatever that meant. I was starting to hear terms such as 'I am not going to have my children hacked to death' or 'I am not going to be butchered in my bed', serious stuff coming from your mother. It was the first time I was to see a soldier with a machine gun called a Bren gun. There had been some problems and soldiers were sent to guard white schools for a time.

Rhodesia was by some called God's Own Country, and I suppose if you wanted to wander around the bush shooting game or just having adventures, it was. Southern Rhodesia was in the building and development stage; as a people they, the whites, were by the very nature of the time and place trekkers, adventurers and pioneers.

Rhodesia had incredible rainy seasons unlike Britain that had constant drizzle. It would be wonderfully hot through the day, then at about three o'clock in the afternoon you could see enormous black clouds building up on the horizon, which would then roll across the sky and dump life-saving rain onto the parched bush, coming down in torrents. The sweet smell of the storm as it hosed down the parched African veldt is a smell and fragrance that is beyond description or explanation. Like the cry of the fish eagle, some things are almost sacred in their inability to be reproduced. You could smell the sweetness of the rain long before it arrived; if you were up on the high ground, you would be able to see the rain falling in sheets, trailing behind a dense purple cloud mass. Then after two or three hours, it would stop, the sky would clear to that fresh bright blue, and everything would be clean and rejuvenated.

My mother believed that Rhodesia was a man's country with little to offer a woman and no future at all for children. Was she a clairvoyant? I don't think so; I think she was just a woman who had known insecurity in her younger days and recognized the signs of potential danger. Not being at all spiritual or religious, I thought this was somewhat magnanimous of God; to let us have free run of the place without any interference from Him. I was, after all a male, so things looked very bright to me, being one who thought a lot about adventure. The country seemed full of healthy suntanned young schoolgirls, one of whom I had a crush on at school. And robust tanned men who wore khaki shorts with long socks folded around their ankles and desert boots. With a pack of thirty cigarettes in the top shirt pocket cut to just the right size to accommodate the pack. On Friday afternoons we would ride into Salisbury proper, meet my mother and father and Sharon, the bikes would go in the boot of the Chevy, then off to the drive-in movies. There we would eat copious amounts of ice cream and biltong (jerky), which everyone would go and buy at intermission from the kiosk right in the centre of the drive-in. You would always bump into someone you knew at intermission. Rhodesia was a big country, but its white population was never large. You could have squished the whole population of 296,000 into a couple of modern sports stadiums. The smallness of the white population was highlighted in the war years when everyone knew someone who had been killed or wounded.

Then there was the real movie house in the centre of Salisbury, the Palace. Its entrance looked more like a theatre, very grand and opulent, with lots of wood panelling and ornate lights. There were full bars and restaurants with waiters who wore white gloves. It even had phone booths on one side and carpeted floors all over the place, plus a men's bar for men only, no ladies allowed. Mother was right; this was a man's country. The film would have an intermission halfway, or first show a newsreel that was flown in from England, all very British and Rule Britannia, before the main feature. Everyone would go to the bar or lounge for a drink or two and socialize. Then a bell would ring, and everyone trooped back inside to watch the film. People used to dress up to the nines; I even saw men in tuxedos, and the ladies often wore long gowns. Going to the movies was not just going to a film; it was a real social occasion, and not only a social event, but it was for many a formal affair, a night out on the town. Africa was in many regards a raw, rough, even dangerous continent. This gathering was for many a golden thread or umbilical cord to civilization. Most English speakers still referred to England as home and when communicating were more English than the English.

Mother started to talk about Australia and the people she knew who had gone there. She had known a lot of Australians in the last war. And me? Well, all I was thinking of was how long would it be before I could get a real rifle so I could go hunting like some of the boys at school who would go home to their family farms during the holidays then come back to school with fantastic stories of hunting with their older brothers, fathers and uncles. Young boys in their teens, and younger, had shot elephant, I mean real elephant.

I must have been about 11 years old when the bombshell got dropped, no consultation; as was the case with the big move to Rhodesia: Would I like to go halfway around the world to an African country, would I behave, work hard at school? to encourage me. This time round no consultation, not even a vague suggestion of it; this time round it was serious stuff: this was a Royal Decree. One day we had a house, the next it was on the market. Whether it got sold or not, I don't know. Pots and pans and other essential equipment were once more packed, labelled and ready. How did she know to keep the sea trunks? Same suitcases and boxes; mind you, eighteen months or two years is not a long time in the grander scheme of things.

We were out of there faster than a cat could run a rat up a drain pipe. I think the turning point came when one day a mob of blacks surrounded a car with a woman and child inside; she was trying to get away, but the rioters were lifting the wheels of her vehicle off the ground. My father commandeered one of the three-ton trucks off-site where he was working then drove down with an Italian or Portuguese friend and broke up the mob so that the woman could drive away. This episode, along with the snake in the garden, was the last straw that pushed the 'let's leave now before it's too late' button. We missed the rush. The return trip to England was a mirror image of our going out to Southern Rhodesia. Bilbo Baggins just about sums it all up with his 'There and back again to see how far it is'. Right now, I was a very cross little boy with the move back to England and deeply disappointed almost to the point of humiliation. Would

I be going back to the same place I had left? Two years was just like an extended vacation.

We as a family had been subject to Mother's command, to move where we would be safe and have some security. In Rhodesia, she would say, 'It doesn't matter where you go, you have dirty brown eyes always looking and watching.' I don't know what they were looking for, but Mum wasn't happy about it. My African adventure was coming to a close. It would resume later. After I had been taught my profession in distant lands – to kill and blow shit up. My family would not learn first-hand of the brutality of the black man and his *Uhuru* that I was to experience later in this Africa I had loved.

We would be safe but not at all that happy. The term 'cold, wet and miserable', all with attitude, took on new meaning. To say our arrival back in England was greeted with inclement weather would be an understatement. Our salutation was a never-ending misty rain, called in the English lexicon drizzle, which was to last for several days. Drizzle, although light, has no benefit whatsoever when you have to walk around in it, especially with luggage to catch a train or stand to get a bus. When shopping for warm, weatherproof clothing, even the shop floors get soaking wet with the backwards and forwards of rain-sodden feet. One's feet, no matter how hard one tries to keep dry, inevitably get damp and cold. Grey misty rain gets down your neck and through anything called a jacket unless it's proper wet-weather gear that mariners use. Our return to England was a revelation. I now understand why the British are such unhappy people; they never see the sun. I recall one of the first things we bought was a pair of long trousers for Keith. They were grey, durable and warm. Strangely enough, we had travelled halfway around the world to buy these trousers at a small Indian shop from an Indian gentleman who had fled Uganda, another African country. Ironic. Drizzle clouded out the sun for days at a time. Knees knocking together with cold hands in pockets, I wondered what had I done this time to deserve this.

We headed north by train to Derbyshire, an uneventful trip. I did not go back to Stalag 17. Apart from continuously wiping the windows of the train to see past the condensation gathering on the glass. We travelled through the drizzle that was a blanket over the length and breadth of the UK. My parents duly found a house to live in, I think rented. Father got a job with Rolls-Royce as he was not prepared to go back into construction. Because of the bad weather, he got a job inside; I had no idea what he did. I recall he went into the hospital for a time, something to do with the war years. It was strange seeing him going off to work riding a bicycle. Other than blacks and schoolchildren, everyone in Rhodesia drove big motor vehicles. I went through the go-back-to-school thing. Keith and I attended the same school for a short time where he was too meet the girl he would later marry.

I moved to yet another school. This entailed walking to my new school alone and introducing myself. 'Hi, I am Rob, where do I sit?' No bicycle ride, we were a one-bicycle family. It was not so bad, I was bigger, more confident and travelled and I had killed snakes in a bucket in Africa.

I had a brief encounter where I discovered the only power a person has over you is the power you give them. I was to report down to the headmaster with another pupil. I was not a big person at that age, but I had a rage inside me, which projected itself whenever I got mad. The Russians say, 'People rage with the pack, but the loner has the rage of the pack inside of him.' The other boy, Walls, was in the head's office at the same time with me. 'Put out your hand, Brown' were the first words I heard. Then, with all his strength that screwed up his face until you could see the veins pumping on the side of his neck, he gave me the hardest caning of my life on my hand with a bamboo cane. Walls just took off out the door in fright – it was his turn next – yelling, 'You're not going to hit me like that!' He just shot out the office. My punishment was three on each hand, but Walls's bolting kind of interrupted the proceedings. When the head told me again, 'Hand out Brown. Other one', I told him he was out of his mind. What with the other boy's bolt to freedom, the headmaster had lost control. He was speechless, the little veins on the side of the head going ninety to the dozen. If ever a headteacher was on his way to a stroke, it had to be him. This short interlude brought about by the unexpected gave me time to get away. I was a truculent youth who had murder in his heart, and he could see it. Believe it or not, all he said to me as I headed for the door was 'At least you took your punishment like a man, Brown.' All I thought was 'You xxxx!' I never used that kind of language, did I. Mother had been right all along: I was a horrible, horrible child. These were the last altercations I would have in England as a child. I had not grown in size, or very little; I was still short and stumpy but I had aged through travel and grown in self-confidence. I was maturing at an early age; I think mutating would be the more descriptive word. If I had been a horrible child, I would turn into a very unpleasant young adult.

I would say our move to Australia was a foregone conclusion, hence our return to the UK. When emigrating, one can only do so from one's country of origin. We had immigrated first to Rhodesia; it was not possible to migrate from Rhodesia to Australia. It would appear our move to Australia was well planned and motivated due to the situation that was seen by my mother as untenable and entirely unacceptable. Maybe there is such a thing as feminine intuition or the survival instinct of the mother for her cubs.

Chapter 3

Australia and Laos: The War that Never Was

If it was so, it might be,
And if it were so, it would be
But as it isn't, it ain't. That's logic.

Lewis Carroll, *Alice Through*
the Looking Glass

The move to Australia was imminent; I wish I could say I was as thrilled as when we moved to Rhodesia, but in two years much water had run under the bridge. It would be correct to mention that some of that water had washed up rose-lipped maidens of tender age. Australia beckoned, but so did a hot little number called Sue who was a bus ride away. A bus ride was costing slightly more than one and ha'pence but well worth the expenditure. Today she may be a grandmother, plump and round, but then she was what one would call a right corker. In my mind, I was to give up something or someone I thought I loved. Time had moved faster than anticipated. It had raced ahead like a greyhound on the track towards that fateful date when I would clamber up the gangplank, to pastures greener. Drab wet England had developed into what was now my life. Full of graceful, long-legged young girls in short skirts with red, pink or rose-petal lips, who spent endless hours going to the powder room together, giggling and discussing who knows what. Was I going to give all this up, for another attempt at another new life? I already had a life, watching pubescent women running back and forth to the powder room.

Children were Australia's primary interest: to restock the gene pool. Oz was a country that had more sheep than people – 14 million souls – at that time. I would go to Australia with the thought of coming back to collect my leggy teenage nightclub dancer. Had you been a gambling man or what they call a bookie, knowing I had never spent more than two years in any one place, any bet on my return would have been easy money, a sure thing. As General MacArthur once said, 'I'll be back' (or was that the Terminator?). My brother would stay in England to get married and come out to Australia later. I had the departure date; I would spend quality time with my girlfriend. Then one evening, the last with her, I just caught a bus and went home. Bizarre really, a bit like going down the road for a packet of fags and never returning. Before departing, there was lots of 'I'll wait for you, write every day, and I miss you so much already' – with a definite hint of déjà vu.

Keith was to stay behind. He seemed so much more mature than me, acting and looking so much older than he was. I had not given Keith much thought in my life, outside of our short bike trips when in Rhodesia, all these counted on one hand. Little brothers tend to embarrass older siblings, especially if they are trying to be cool with their friends. We did not do a lot together. Knowing he would stay in England, why could I not also? I did not want to leave, and I most certainly did not want to leave him behind. He was my brother; would I ever see him again?

England was embarking on the Swinging Sixties, an era of Mary Quant, the Beatles, Mini cars and even smaller miniskirts on leggy girls with Twiggy hairstyles and boots that strippers would look good in, along with Christine Keeler and Mandy Rice-Davies. Great Britain was about to blossom, and I was leaving it all behind; I was going to miss it all, for gum trees and bloody marsupials. In retrospect Irene, my mother, got it right this time; I think more by good luck than in-built sound judgment, or through some clairvoyant ability to see into the future.

Keith did marry his schoolgirl sweetheart and now lives in Australia. Did he find success? I think Keith's success lay in the fact that he had three children, two girls, and a boy. His children hung around at home; rather than go to a friend's house, the friends would come to theirs. It was a warm place where people interacted. I think Keith was a good father and was close to his children. They were a family; I believe this is a success.

My sister Sharon also benefited from the Australian move, marrying and having a close family; she runs a family tour business with her husband and girls. All up, I have to give it to Irene; she found a place of safety for her children. I fell through the cracks. Someone told me my parents did the best with what they had. My response was that they could have done better, but there again, I was a nasty bit of work: ask my Mum.

Very rarely as a child did I see my father throw a pity party for the horrors life had dealt so many of his generation. Many came back missing an arm, a leg or their eyesight, yet they carried on. I recall one of these grumpy old men attacked me at my place of employment in Australia. He just up and started to punch me. I concede I could be a bit difficult from time to time, but this seemed just a little extreme, seeing as I did not even know him. When called to the supervisor's office, he asked me what I had done or said. My response was, 'I don't know.' My attacker had been a Japanese prisoner of war. On the island of Singapore he spent weeks in the notorious Changi prison, being tortured and almost starved to death. Then he was sent north to the infamous Burma railway; I mean, who wouldn't be more than a little pissed off with the world after all of that.

I can only recall having anything that resembles a conversation with my father twice in my life. Before leaving to do my basic parachute course, I asked what it was like to jump out of an aeroplane. I got a vague response: 'You either do it, or you don't.' I had expected something with a little more depth. When he was flying around over Germany at night waiting to be shot up, or down, I thought he might have had time to ponder his fate when and if he had to bail out. Maybe a little light humour from him at that time would have gone a long way, something akin to 'It's better jumping out with a parachute than without one.' I also recall him telling me, 'Never go to war, son; stay at home and make money and let the other silly bugger do the fighting.' This, of course, was not a conversation as such, but it was wisdom. Wisdom wasted on a young boy in his early teens whose hormones were bouncing off the wall with an all-consuming, healthy interest in trying to get his hands down some equally inexperienced girl's knickers. Why would he think I would be thinking of war?

The Australian digger has always acquitted himself well in battle, mostly fighting for a dead thing called the Empire. Taking the size of its population into account, Australia as a nation and its military have done remarkably well when called on to travel and fight over vast distances. The average Australian digger would never have met or sat and had a beer with the people giving the orders, that is the people in government. If he had he would more than likely have disliked them more than his enemy. Australians do not have a very high regard for wallies (slow and not very bright), politicians, authority, child molesters and anyone who is cruel to their dog or does not pay for his round of beers. Australians are identifiable by a lack of subtlety, political correctness and diplomacy, words that did not appear in the Australian lexicon when I was growing up. Australia was a better place for it. People told the truth; unfortunately, the new world order managed somehow to squeeze through the cracks and before you knew it, the Australian digger was not allowed to call a spade a spade. He has no time for the UN, politicians and that magic group called VIPs. Is he not understanding just how significant these people think they are to the world?

The Australian military had not been to war since Korea; although small contingents were doing something somewhere at some time, such as Malaya or Borneo. The rest of Australia would not have known about it or been remotely interested, what with not being able to take with them a surfboard, football or cricket bat. Knowing what I knew, or did not know, why would I be thinking of war or the military? The world liked us; we were good at rugby and cricket, not that I personally ever played either of these games. We also had super surfing, and the Sheilas weren't half-bad either. So why would we, or I, go to war? It would involve much travelling. We would have to travel miles to find someone to fight. Australia is a massive island and if someone wanted to fight us the same would apply. Just too much travelling time when we could be doing something we liked doing.

My mother often shouted at my father, 'Put him in the army, Alf; he's never going to amount to much.' This attitude pointed to the fact that when it came to the military my parents held different points of view; in fact, they were diametrically opposite. My father had told me in no uncertain terms to avoid uniform, i.e. war; my mother, however, had no problem turning me into a child soldier and sending me off to who knows where and to an unknown fate. The military never entered our home or my mind; why would it? we had no one to fight. I might have dreamed of being a Spitfire pilot once. That was more along the lines of a kid dreaming of driving a fire engine, never really seeing past the big red truck and the shiny bell.

So, if the military was not my thing, why was I standing at the edge of a wooden pier looking down into the cold, murky waters of Port Phillip Bay in mid-winter? Holding a length of iron bar, supposedly the same weight as a rifle and an old pair of boots slung around my neck in soaking-wet JGs (jungle greens) that had up until a short time ago been worn by another witless victim. You may have heard the story of the two cobbers who went and joined the army just for a bit of a prank. The two of them sign up then do the medical and the one who suggested this game is declared medically unfit. Meantime, his mate is whisked away into the army. For all his protestations he is in and no one is interested in 'What about my mate? it was his idea.' My story is similar but not quite.

Flanagan (aka Flip) was all of six foot, older than me by ten years if not more. He told the most fantastic war stories; you know the bloke that everyone listens to, admires and likes. I could only have been about 16 then. Flip was the epitome of the Australian digger. He had rifles and pistols and things in his workshop that made it look like an Aladdin's cave. He was what would be termed a 'prepper', a survivalist in today's parlance. A real action man and could he pull the Sheilas. Flanagan had acquired a new girlfriend called Paddy. She was a pleasant person; I liked her. Paddy was a teacher in a small school up in the hills past a place called Ferntree Gully. As it happened, Paddy had a girlfriend who taught in the same school. Life can, from time to time, be most convenient and accommodating. Celeste was about seven years older than me, in her early twenties. I started to go out with her. I was too young to have a driving licence and had no vehicle. Celeste used to drive this little green car, a Mini. For a 16-year-old, I was having the time of my life. Rest assured, the lady did not leave me mentally scarred for life and wondering where my youthful innocence had gone. In this regard, every woman I went out with after Celeste should have sent her a thank–you note or a commendation. I learned a lot from her and why not? She was after all a teacher. I can honestly say, outside of my profession, women, especially beautiful, bright, intelligent women, have schooled me in the better virtues of life, more than any man has. Each woman has, in turn, taught me about compassion, art, music and more. I had never seen a live stage show until I met Celeste, never taken a woman out to a candlelit dinner or ordered wine or opened a door for a woman. Women have been incredible mentors to me throughout life. They have taught and imbued me with an appreciation for good food, art, history and so much more; that there's no shame or embarrassment to be moved by good music. Special Forces instructors teach you how to kill, survive and to destroy.

This time was a time of learning for me. I had Flip and his guns and hunting and bushwalking and all the macho digger stuff as well as getting fit. Then he told me he was going to get married to Paddy. I liked Paddy; after all, she had introduced me to Celeste. Then she started to put on weight and Flip became a father. The guns and hunting were put on the backburner 'only for a short time, mate'.

I was still going out with my twenty-something femme fatale, living in Celeste's private little world of art, music and the more beautiful things. When not with Flip, I was with her learning how not to splash food all over the white tablecloth. I would not say my world ended with one sudden, violent bang but come to an end it did, or maybe just being very young, I thought it was ending. I was about to find out what the term a lifestyle change meant. She wanted to go somewhere nice and have dinner; we hadn't got halfway through the meal when she told me at the end of her school term, she was going overseas for a year. She would be back; it was only a year and she would write. Now where had I heard that before? This year was turning out to be a disastrous year for me. Celeste was more than just my mistress or lover; she was my life coach, a beautiful, woman, a wonderful friend.

Soon after Celeste left Ferntree Gully so did I. I did all right in Sydney, living on the Cross in a flat on Darlinghurst Road, right in the middle of King's Cross selling paintings for a pom called Austin who was an artist and spoke with a strange accent. Being a real artist with paint all over bits of his clothing, he used to pull the Sheilas. I lied and told people it was my artwork, made lots of money and also pulled the Sheilas. I was now going out with someone my age who thought I was frightfully, frightfully experienced. Well done, Celeste. I found out everything she had taught me worked wonderfully well. My girlfriend, whatever her name was, also talked with a strange posh accent and was, at the tender age of 16, Lady Something or Other from some obscure peerage in Wales or somewhere, but she swore like a trooper, smoked dope and liked surfing and had a fantastic little body. It was that wonderful time when women went onto the contraceptive pill. To prove that they were liberated and could screw as much if not more than any man could. Who was I to deny them the opportunity to show it to be so?

It was time for Celeste to come home. I returned to Melbourne. The Beatles had become famous. I no longer used hair cream or dressed like Elvis Presley. I had matured somewhat and found I could survive on my own. If I had learned back in the UK that people only have the power over you that you give them, in Australia, I discovered I did not need people to survive. Celeste did come home but not back to me; she had changed as much as I had. She had met and was going to marry someone overseas. It never happened – but for us, it ended.

So, what did I want to do with my life? I had given up a good little business selling my or Austin's paintings to come back to Celeste who would just become a memory. I was paging through a newspaper and came across an advertisement for the military. It was a well-put-together collage of photos showing parachuting, diving and roping down a cliff, all the stuff that Flip had done. Being curious, I went and asked him how difficult it was, this thing called selection. He told me I would not be able to do it for various reasons, too small, not fit enough, etc. He was more than a little blunt. A bit like my dad is bigger than your dad. One of my hurdles other than the fitness was being legally a minor. I had to get a consent form signed by my father.

Had he succumbed to my mother's years of propaganda? 'Put him into the army, Alf.' I contacted the advertiser to get the date for the next pre-selection fitness course. One does not acquire that kind of fitness in two or three weeks. Flanagan was proved right about fitness. That's why I was standing on the edge of a wooden pier looking down into the freezing, murky waters of Port Phillip Bay in mid-winter, clothed in soggy jungle greens. Someone yelled 'Go!' so I went. My feet hit the freezing water. I sank with little possibility of swimming. I went down and down. I was going to die. If the surface view of Port Philip Bay that day looked uninviting, dark, menacing and murky, once under the water, it became even more so; I could see absolutely nothing. My arms were going like windmills in a desperate attempt to keep afloat; all and any idea of swimming abandoned to panic as I went down like a lead weight: this was an exercise in survival not a pre-selection for fitness. The boots around my neck were there, so, should I be able to stay on the top and swim, I would be entangled, eliminating any chance of staying alive, my death assured and imminent. The sole purpose of the iron bar was to send me immediately to Davy Jones's Locker by embedding my feet in the muddy bottom of the bay at high velocity. Should I drop the iron bar? Would they indeed make me pay for it, as had been suggested? 'This is like your rifle; if you lose it you pay for it.' What of the boots – old and soaking wet agreed, but still the property of the Australian Army? If I lost them would I have to replace them or, horror upon horror, be forced to get back into the water to retrieve them should I live through the ordeal? All of a sudden, a hand grabbed me by the hair and pulled me to the surface. I would live, although at that time I did not think so. I went away somewhat dejected. I had failed the swimming test.

I had no idea that it would take so much effort to join the army. My mother's cry of 'Put him the army, Alf' had somehow instilled in me the idea that the military is made up of the dregs of failed humanity. There was nowhere else to put them. They would not let me have another go, and I could not continue with the other fitness tests. The Australian Commandos were not only parachute soldiers but also, in no small degree, waterborne. Meaning if you could not swim, you had a genuine chance of becoming a floater – long before you got anywhere to help break things and do your job as was explained to me. Once drowned, you became pretty useless for any task given.

I had not told anyone I was trying for pre-selection, so no significant loss of face. I walked away after being told I could go over the fence to another unit. I replied, 'No thanks, I came to get into the Commandos.' I was halfway down the pier when a voice yelled at me, 'Get back here, you little bastard.' I was told to go away and train, then come back in six months and have another go at drowning. So, I spent the next six months running and swimming, and still no one had any idea I had tried but failed, and even less of an idea that I was training to have another attempt. I had no idea why I kept going and even less of an idea of what waited for me. Maybe it was the possibility of getting lots of free stuff and a real rifle that held some appeal.

I almost drowned at my next attempt. Almost, but I was fitter and kept on going; helping hands pulled me up, and I went with the magic group that had survived. I managed to do the entire programme of fitness tests. I looked around; there weren't many of us left to go forward with the next phase, a solid three-week selection course. I lost my toenails with all the running and forced twenty-kilometre marches along with a great deal of weight. I had no clue as to what I was doing; I had imagined, after listening to Flip's stories, it sounded like fun. For saying I knew nothing, I took to soldiering, enjoying the jungle training and found soldiering came easily. Laying ambush sites, demolitions and guerrilla warfare were right up my alley. On my demolitions course, blowing shit up and breaking things, I set charges on an old railway line and when the Warrant Officer II (WOII) instructor came around, he said, 'Very nice, very nice indeed' with much the same voice as an admirer of beautiful artwork, or a critic of excellent food. He then finished with 'You do have a nasty little mind. You're going be a nasty bit of work.' I think he knew my mum. I had found my rightful place in the world. I was good at what I did.

I did my basic parachute course at RAAF Williamstown Fort Gellibrand in New South Wales. The Australians at that time did not have a parachute battalion or even a company for that matter. They had an airborne platoon for demonstrations. That's what it is called a demonstration platoon. I suppose you have to stay within budget and work with what you have. Out of 14 million people, a platoon is all they could scrape together. I spoke with one of them, a Vietnam vet. I asked him what it was like and he explained he had spent a whole year doing patrols and never once saw a thing. I was to find out later that's the way it can be at times: it's all or nothing. Years later I knew a young recruit who completed selection and became a badged SAS member; on his first (and only) operation he got shot in the head – dead – all or nothing at times.

I had no idea what parachuting would be like. You're in the aircraft, someone opens a door and you fall out. The military can often surprise you. Three days into my parachute course, I had still not seen a parachute, nor could I stand up straight. I discovered stomach muscles and leg muscles I never knew I had. Roll left, roll right, feet and knees together, front roll, side left, side right roll, and 'feet, feet, keep your legs and feet together'. You had to be deformed to get into the landing positions asked for; we bent our bodies and legs into the most grotesque angles. Actions and drills for when landing in trees and obstacles, actions for water descents, over and over ad nauseam. The fan tower jump: downnnnnnnn you go, feet and knees together with that never-ending voice shouting encouragement. 'Look up, kick twists out and fly your reserve!' Instructions and actions for when it worked and when it did not, which made one wonder, after being told the canopies always opened. An endless string of new words and commands, actions learned until it was no longer an ordeal but a smooth-flowing activity, almost normal, or as normal as leaving a perfectly serviceable aeroplane hundreds of feet above the ground can be. Something one did without even thinking. The term 'Action stations' would resound in my head from that time up to the present. The military has an action drill for everything. The training was hard and superb; no one was going to die parachuting. In the training hangar maybe but not parachuting – crippled perhaps, but not dead, not on their watch. The leg and stomach pains subsided through constant hammering, training and use. Then one magical day you are all kitted up and checking your rig; you can smell the avgas (aviation fuel) and hear the deep drone as the plane is warming up the engines just outside, the smell permeating the loading area, with a fragrance that goes inside your head. Working its way into the heart of every parachute soldier who has ever walked across that hard standing and boarded the waiting trooper. A noise and aroma that will stay and live with you for the rest of life, a smell so overpowering that it will often be recalled with a shudder or a cynical smile.

The first jump, or 'lob', is clean fatigues, i.e. with no equipment, and a 'chalk' (a stick) of two bodies in daylight hours, ordinarily in the early morning before any wind or drift gets up. You're over the DZ before you know it. Then the yelling from the dispatcher: 'Stand up, hook up, check equipment.' You go through the drills, only this time with more skill; it's a long way down. The tail end of the de Havilland Canada DHC-4 Caribou twin-engine troop carrier slowly opens as the rear of the aeroplane floor lowers into a ramp. You shuffle to the slope; you can see the ground now and wonder if you have forgotten anything when you did your equipment check. You do a shuffle closer to the aperture on 'Action stations'. The dispatcher calls, 'Red on'. You're staring up at the red light and wait; you're like a young thoroughbred waiting for the gate to fly open so you can start the race. Its green, it's green, how long has it been green? You have not been watching for a millisecond, and all you hear is 'Go!' You never listened to the dispatcher yelling 'Reds on, reds on, greens on, go, go, go!' You exit so fast, and you're relieved to get out that damned aircraft. Then, if all goes well, you are floating and take in the wonder of it all. It ends too soon, the ground coming up, someone talking through a loud hailer, feet, feet, get them together, knees together, feet up, knees bent, chin in! The last few feet a rush, then you hit, you roll feet and knees together, the roll takes the ground down the side of your legs and across your upper back, and you are down. You are now up on your feet and have the most unmistakeable, the stupidest clownlike grin on your face that the world has ever seen. You're a parachute soldier.

I later specialized in small-scale raids, and water work and diving. I was never a happy diver, although today I am a registered professional divemaster and enjoy my diving. Due to my poor education, I struggled with sea navigation; we had no GPS then and it was all maths, slide rule charts and tidal flows. I did qualify, and my report recommended me for further specialist training. Our training area for most of our boat work was at Port Philip Bay and Wilson's Promontory, an area best described as isolated and inhospitable that included every possible type of terrain – mountains, forest as dense any tropical jungle, mudflats, sand dunes and swamp; in fact, everything any swimmer canoeist could ask for. Port Philip Bay is an area of water that is unforgiving and dangerous; if you don't know what you're doing, and even if you do, it can claim your life before you even know it's happening. The Rip or Heads is the most treacherous stretch of sea in Australia; it connects the Bass Strait and Port Phillip Bay. It is a 3.2-kilometre-wide body of water between Point Nepean and Point Lonsdale in Victoria. The Bay proper is an area of more than 1,900 square kilometres; that's a lot of sea to play around on, or under, or to get lost in and drowned. It's a reality, especially with Special Forces, that training is hard, demanding, and many times we pushed the envelope, sometimes ending in tragedy. It's not through lousy planning. You can't tease and poke the horseman's white horse and expect to get away with it all the time. Shit happens; it should not, but it does.

A narrow entrance governs the tidal range in the bay, and the water flowing in and out through the Rip. It has tidal flows that run at up to 15 km/h through this narrow channel between reefs and across a rock shelf. The Rip, or the Heads, is known to have claimed some thirty ships and severely damaged many more. Its hazardous waters have claimed several hundred lives. In February 1960, a few short years before I became a member of 2 Commando, 2 Commando held a waterborne training exercise; the raiding party would traverse the bay area and put in their attack. The group consisted of seventy-four commandos, almost the whole commando. The raiders went in using two-man kayaks. They were caught by a strong tidal flow that pushed them out through the Rip into the open sea where they faced ten-metre-high waves. The rough seas capsized the canoes and the amphibious vehicles. Many of the men were picked up by larger rescue boats which in turn were overturned, once again dumping them back into the heavy seas. A warrant officer and the driver of an amphibious vehicle drowned. Some of the commandos were rescued in the Straits after being picked up by a ship. Another commando was lost when swept away by a massive wave.

We also had climbing fatalities. A rope was attached to a tow hitch on a vehicle; the climber was halfway up the climbing tower and the rope was sagging. To give it a bit more tension to make the climb easier, the 4x4 took up the slack in the line and it snapped like a cotton thread; the rock ape came straight down: he died in hospital. It sounds as if we were clumsy or just slack with safety. The commando units were very young and feeling their way. Often, we were experimenting – suck it and see kind of thing.

When I did my diving course, I almost became a victim, lost at sea. I was doing a compass night dive with a buddy. In those days we did not have underwater torches nor would we have used them anyway: a torch underwater is easily seen, especially from the air unless you're having to swim through silt or very think mud. Apart from that, I don't believe torches were sealed to withstand water pressure: for every metre you go down, you increase the pressure by one bar or 14.7 pounds per inch. So, we dived with no torch. We sat on the side of the rubber boat; it was a straightforward exercise. Get in, go down, compass swim on to target, do the job, come up, go home. Diving at night we would tether ourselves to a float with an Esko light on it, a little lamp activated by saltwater; the safety launch – a yellow speedboat called the *Yellow Pearl* – would follow the light bobbing around on the raft. When we finished, we would surface on the float. So, I went in and my buddy followed, took a bearing then went down and did what divers do. We swam and swam, expecting to reach the target. Once on target, the rubber boat would pull us up, and we could all go home. However, on the top side, our float and light were heading off towards the Rip. The safety boat tried to pull us up only to find they had no divers on the end of the rope. Panic: they had lost two divers. Meanwhile, we were swimming into shallow water. The first I knew we had trouble was when I felt as if someone or something was trying to lift my almost empty tanks off my back. I lifted my head to try and stop the tanks from swimming around. As I lifted my head, it broke surface; we were so shallow our tanks were on top of the water and every time a wave came in it lifted us bodily like someone using a bodyboard. We had swum up onto the beach and were lying face down in about a foot of water. There before us shone the bright lights of St Kilda. We had a problem: we had lost the boat or the boat had lost us. It was now trawling somewhere out on Port Philip Bay looking for two divers who they thought might be heading for the Rip. We climbed out of the water and went looking for someone, so we could radio back and say 'Hi, come and get us.' You can't walk miles in the diving kit; well you can, but St Kilda is a bustling place, and in those days a red light area and you got tired saying no thank you or explaining why you were walking along the road trying to bum a lift dressed like a frog. We found a police car and they radioed the launch. I thought we were in the shit for this one. I have never seen a sergeant-major so happy to see wayward troops in my whole time in the military. Two prodigal sons lost to the Rip, but now we were found.

One of the tasks of military divers is to swim up large soil outlet pipes full of poo or sludge to locate demolitions placed by bad people or under and around ships in silt, mud or other appalling conditions. The army lost me as a diver due to the fact I never had one dive where I could see anything; it was always dark with poor visibility, cold and, naturally, wet. The best part about diving was being picked up by the rubber boats.

A swimmer canoeist would sometimes surface-swim in without tanks to do a job, then surface-swim out to a given point for pick-up. The team would line up on the surface, spaced about a hundred metres apart with just your head above water. A high-speed rubber boat would aim straight for your head, the wake or bow wave would hit you first and push you down one side of the rubber boat, a hoop would go over your arm, which had been held above the water and the momentum would swing you up and into the 10-Z duck. That was fun.

For small-scale raids, we trained first in original Second World War canoes that had the flotation device external to the mainframe. They were stout and extremely seaworthy, being able to take heavy surf and high seas. Sometime later we would get Klepper canoes. I was always cold, wet and muddy. We would row all night and end up with blisters the size of golf balls on our hands. Our hands would become soft from being wet for so long and, after a few hours, all you could see was a mass of raw skin. It was okay as long as you kept rowing. If you stopped for any length of time your fingers would just seize and cramp up and not be able to hold the paddle again; the answer to this was when you stopped rowing not to uncurl your fingers and hands from around the paddle. After hours of this we would then have to LUP (lay-up) and camouflage the boats, dragging the kayak through mud and swamps or over unfriendly terrain. Strangely, this I enjoyed.

I qualified fully as a commando and was awarded my wings and green beret. The UK commando units are the Royal Marines and are highly trained infantry and waterborne troops. I had the privilege of soldiering with some of them later, both in Rhodesia and Iraq. However, Australia's commandos are army, but we also played in the water.

Units formed in the Second World War now disbanded at the end of hostilities, having performed and served their countries well. This loss of expertise led to a downgrading and removal of skills and intellectual integrity. The Australian military reverted to the concept held in prewar years, that of supplying Australian troops under Commonwealth defence arrangements, primarily supporting the British Empire. After 1945, the Australians lost most of its Special Forces capability. It was only through the far-sightedness of Lieutenant-General Sir Henry Wells that Australia would revive its SF role in the 1950s. The political climate after the Second World War dictated that many units would go. The Long-Range Desert Group and the Special Air Service suffered that very fate. It was only the Malayan emergency of 1948–1960 and the forming of the Malayan Scouts that would mutate into the present Special Air Service we know today, that saved the SAS from extinction.

With regards to the war in the Far East during the Second World War, the Australians had for some time been formulating and preparing for war in the jungles of Asia. The British had formed and dispatched to Melbourne in October 1940 Task Force 104 to raise Special Forces independent commando companies. By early 1941, it had selected a training location in the state of Victoria at the southern tip of Australia called Wilson's Promontory. This vast, uninhabited area included every kind of rugged topography to test any SF recruit. Task Force104 completed its mission of establishing a jungle warfare school in July 1941 and handed over the training to the Australians, some five months before the attack on Pearl Harbor of 7 December 1941. The school's official designation in the early years was the 7th Infantry Training Centre Guerilla Warfare School. As mentioned, Wilson's Promontory would later become 2 Commando's training ground. There was also the Jungle Warfare School at Canungra, Queensland, formed in 1942. It is still operational today and the leading jungle training school for all infantry troops.

In the 1950s the Australians reconstituted 1 Commando in Sydney, New South Wales, and 2 Commando in Melbourne, Victoria. The Australian Special Air Service was formed in 1957 as a company. My instructors were Second World War, Korean and Malayan veterans. I became a commando only twenty-one short years after the end of the war, and only fifteen short years after my unit's inception. I joined a special forces unit that was in its infancy. Although the group itself was young, the training I received was excellent and would save my life many times in many parts of the world. I was and still am very proud of being a member of 2 Commando in Australia, and that my military journey began with them. Being on the Pacific Rim, Australians are world-renowned jungle operators. My instructors were men like Geordia (who went on to win the Military Medal in Vietnam), Nowak and Warrant Officer Jimmy Hubbard, men who undoubtedly provided the superb training that was to save my life time after time.

One of the most devastating things to take place concerning my friendship with Flip and Paddy was when I got a lift with an old army mate who knew Flip. The conversation got on to Flanagan and what he had done. The next words that came out of this old digger's mouth were 'The lying bastard; he never left Australia.' Now, from all that I had heard, I had assumed Flanagan had been on active service. He had not. He had not lied to me; he had just omitted some facts. I felt kind of let down. He had been my boyhood hero.

It was a short time after this, I met and married my first wife. There is an old saying you can tell a special forces soldier by his Rolex watch, divorce papers in the top pocket of his combat fatigues and an indigenous bracelet or amulet from some obscure tribe. Elizabeth came from what the Americans on the East Coast call Old Money, a term my son Guy does not like at all and rejects quite strongly. How do I know that the Jenkins family came from old money? Simple: they told me. They were not nasty about it, but Jesse, Elizabeth's mother, came across a little bit strong on occasion. Her father had been one of the leading medical people in Melbourne, nay, in Victoria. When she first told me the family history, it was appreciated even if unasked for, as I was genuinely interested. I think she expected me to reciprocate but I was not prepared to tell her about old Joe, the rag and bone man. And most certainly no mention of the O'Bryant side of the family. Elizabeth's father Eric was an ex-navy captain; in his day he had been the youngest Australian to be given command of a ship. I am not sure whether this was the Merchant Navy or the find 'em and sink 'em navy. I suspect the latter but either way, I thought that it was quite an achievement. I could have told them about drunken O'Bryant; they would have understood. Jess for all her eccentricities was not challenging to get on with. I thought Eric was pretty neat being a navy captain. There was one glaring problem: Eric was a raging alcoholic. I have always found alcoholics other than the O'Bryant kind to be very agreeable people, not all of them but in general. A lot of them are well educated, witty and articulate when sober. They always seem to know unusual people and have been to fascinating places and done exciting things. Some can quote from Kipling and Shakespeare and recite the St. Crispin Day speech.

Apart from Jess and Eric, of course, I also liked Liz. I had to go and tell Eric that his teenage daughter, not long out of school was pregnant. I was not looking forward to this; it was going to be difficult. How was I going to go about this task? Best bet, tell him straight up. That's what we did in Australia, or so I thought: 'Listen, mate, I knocked up your daughter. Sorry about that. Let's have a beer and what shall we call the little bastard?' Eric was in the kitchen when I broke the news that he was to be a grandfather. He did not take it well. I ducked the punch. Cut a long story short the momentum of his punch put him in a position to be thrown over my shoulder. Then we rolled around on the floor a bit, some yelling and screaming from Jess then it was all over. Now this is strange: I was old enough to be in the army, but I had to get consent to get married. I married Elizabeth Louis Jenkins in uniform. I did not have enough money for a tuxedo or a suit.

Liz looked quite tasty, and in fact, she was a stunning bride being very svelte and did not show. I don't know if Elizabeth loved me. More likely she was just a frightened pregnant teenager. I regret I did not do better. She is one of the people I always wanted to say sorry to. The best part of it was when Guy was born. My son Guy was something else. He was a real little beauty; I have never felt that feeling again like the first time I saw him. Like many firsts there can only be one first of any given thing, the first parachute descent, the first love, the first deep dive, the first contact and the first death. One does not forget firsts in a hurry. I have met some brilliant soldiers, some very young. In Rhodesia, in my world, you had lance-corporals who at an early age were leaders of men, controlling firefights and calling in air support. Yet many times when we are in the real world, or the other world, we are totally irresponsible. We are given toys that are worth a fortune, allowed to blow up bridges that cost millions to rebuild, destroy buildings, take life and kill wholesale. Yet for many of us when it comes to the simple everyday things in this other world, we are total screw-ups. As my sister-in-law once put it, 'Rob, you live on another planet and always have done.' There are many ways to describe my behaviour that destroyed our marriage, some of them obscene, a few humorous, but at the end of the day I just think I was a bloody awful husband.

Australia had committed a small team about thirty advisers to Vietnam in early 1962, long before most Australians even knew there was a war there. Both 1 and 2 Commando sent instructor-advisers. I believe a member of 1 Commando was one of the first Australian VCs in that war. I spoke to Geordia, my sergeant, about going to Vietnam, but trying to get on an advisory team was impossible: I was too inexperienced and too young. The Conscription Act of 1965 dictated you had to be 20 when called up and I had only just turned eighteen. The only way to get to Vietnam was to transfer to the infantry, something that Geordia actually did. Contrary to popular belief, Vietnam had troops lining up at the boss's door to go. Even if I transferred, I would still have to wait. I was seriously considering a transfer to an infantry unit as an option when I had a visit from a friend who had transferred out. He had given up his green beret and got a new hat, one with the turned-up brim on the side. His problem was the battalion he was posted to had just returned from a tour in Vietnam. They would not be going any place any time soon, and neither would he. In the army, you can put in a request for a posting, but that does not necessarily mean you are going to get what you want. They don't always let you decide where you're going to go; they send you where they think you should go. My reasoning at that time was you had to get the timing right; his reply was that it wouldn't work and they could end up sending you to someplace out beyond the black stump, guarding an ammunition dump. From 1965 to 1970 the Australian commitment peaked at around 70,000 troops with just over 63,000 conscripts entering the military; 19,000 would see service in Vietnam. I, in all probability, would not have been one of them.

All militaries have what are called barrack-room lawyers, people who know everything. You will always find someone who knows someone who knew a friend of a friend who did it, and it worked. I discovered my expert digger and was informed that the US Army employed civilians in Vietnam and, being Australian, 'She'll be right mate, you just got to get there; you'll be okay and find a job. You should make good money as well'. If I had signed on and went to an infantry battalion, I might have had a very tentative, and I say a tentative, chance of an overseas posting. The whole thing was too precarious and manipulative. Speaking to others who had been conned and short-changed, the idea of three years beyond the black stump did not appeal to me. The Australians were already talking about a drawdown of troops shortly after my service had finished with 2 Commando.

Years later, in 1977, I met Robby from Australia when I was in the Rhodesian SAS. Robby would be killed in Lebanon fighting for the Christian Maronites. He told me when he was in the Australian Army with an infantry battalion, and he had only about eight months left before the end of his service, his battalion was shipping out to Vietnam. He would be left behind in Australia with what is called a rear party (not everyone ships out, a small rear element is left behind to maintain their area, i.e. stay in Australia) and Robby would demob, end his service time halfway through the overseas tour. They told him if he wanted to get overseas, he had to re-enlist for three years. He wrote to his local Member of Parliament and complained. He got to do his half-tour in Vietnam. Had the MP not got involved most certainly, Robby would have had to stay in Australia to look after the company stores.

I boarded a flight to Singapore. My certificate of service with the Australians showed that I left 2 Commando on the 20 October 1968. My visa for Vietnam stated 'October valid until December' and I had already been in and out of Laos several times.

Laos: North-east of the Mekong River, October 1968

It is 0300. I am enveloped in darkness, seeing little as I crouch down low at the edge of the jungle trying to make out some kind of outline against the skyline, the moon hidden behind the clouds. I have been contracted to take part in what was loosely termed a civil action or psychological operation by some obscure agency, I think mostly due to my being a westerner, and if I disappear no one will look for me. Something I have thought about in the past days and hoped was incorrect. The ground is still wet and the fine powder-like dirt that kicked up to become choking dust in the dry season is now a slippery layer of mud. It clings to my boots and clothing. Rarely is this war reported, if at all. The conflict taking place is in the interior of the country. The media is kept at a distance. It is just as well as the world does not need another Vietnam on the TV.

There should be a village right where I am crouching; I question whether we are in the right place. I can see no silhouettes of huts. I stand up and go forward, my team hunkered down on my flanks invisible in the dark. I am hoping they are awake after our rest. We are all fatigued and under strain from our long march. I move out of cover; the village has to be here or close by. My partner or teammate is very good at directions. We are not lost; we just don't know where we are on the map. I take a few silent steps and leave the jungle edge into what is a clearing. In the dark, I stumble into a hole, a large hole; I am soaking wet now and up to my knees in water. It is neither hot nor cold. The monsoons should be ending soon; there is still a lot of water around due to the rains being a lot heavier than average. We are part of what is called a limited or single objective operation – Hearts and Minds. Gathering and processing information. It is a time-consuming job. At briefings, I am informed they have only ever once lost a team. My heart is racing; even if no one can see me down in the hole, I start to worry about being in an ambush situation. Experience tells me I would already be dead if it were. I can't see the rim of the pit I have fallen into. Where am I? My teammate I think is looking down at me; I don't know as it is still very dark, but I imagine he is.

'Lobby, Lobby, you good?'

'Shut the fuck up or you'll wake the whole world.'

Silence reigns once more. I am trying to get out the hole, which I think is an old a bomb crater. By calling me, the young guide has given me an idea of what direction to move in; I have never been in such total darkness before. I hold my hand up and pull the cover of my watch back; the luminosity jumps out at me, my hand being so close to my face. Down in my bomb crater, I worry about a Vietnamese ambush, or a Pathet Lao ambush, or an anybody ambush. I manage to extricate myself. The two of us are now lying on the edge of the hole out in the open, trying to make out anything that looks remotely like an area that once had life in it. Where are the huts? Reality dawns on me. It appears the village recently had a visit from a B-52 or any one of the many warplanes that dump ordnance on Laos as their secondary target. We move back into the jungle. We will wait for the morning light, and know if we are in the right place or off the map. I sit in the dark, not looking forward to daylight. I have been here before and depending on how long ago the B-52, if it was a B52, dumped its ordnance, will determine the condition of the bodies if there are any left. I move our position back: if there is one crater there would be more, sometimes so deep you have trouble finding your way out. The darkness is receding. I stop. To my front lies a dead, half-naked but still intact body. There is something strange about it. I then notice the top half is on its back looking up at the sky while the bottom half has its legs and feet pointing in the opposite direction. The blast had twisted the body like a corkscrew, how many twists I cannot yet tell. No sign of the village but what stretches out in front of me are holes, big ones and smaller ones and lots of them, but no sign of life, just a decimated jungle clearing.

As the sun comes up, it becomes more humid, and the team fans out. Looking for what? I suppose signs of life, loot that can be picked up and sold on or maybe souvenirs. The area is void of life, and the landscape pockmarked with holes of varying size. Here and there one can kick or fall over some small remnant that suggests life, once upon a time. My line function or mission is to simply observe and report what I see, with the definite instruction to stay out of trouble. It was a long march in, walk and creep, as we patrolled through a jungle of varying density. Now, on my fourth day out, I am starting to feel more confident. Officially, I am not here. I have no idea of the fatigue and strain that will set in later. I am in a surreal world. As I move around, clumps of mud stick to my boots. I am wearing my old commando boots – we called them wobble cobbles, standard boots that we fitted with thick rubber soles. The tread is deep like a tractor tyre and once the mud gets into them, it adds more than a kilo or two. Not the ideal footwear for muddy terrain, but brilliant for mountain or rock work, which in the jungle one does not get a lot of. It goes through my mind I should have taken the boots offered. Voices rise as the men whisper, telling each other there is little danger as the bombs have flattened everything, a testament to the waste and futile expenditure of the all-consuming beast called war.

All that is left now is for us to return, to go back and tell whoever that thousands of US dollars' worth of ordnance has been dumped on miles of jungle, wiping out a village of unknown size. I am sure it won't go down well. The men look bored as the initial fascination of the flattened sight wears off and they move back into the jungle. Something inside of me is screaming a silent scream; they are doing everything wrong. They are acting like tourists, not combatants in a hostile zone. Then it comes, the sickening dull *plop*. I hear the rustling noise as it comes down. I am in a small crater, yelling 'Mortars, take cover' when two troops tumble in alongside me, laughing insanely. Then the bombs stop and I put my head over the side and I can see there are little men dressed in brown to my front in the distance, all running towards Mrs Brown's little boy, trying to kill him. They come from the other side of the flattened village. There are one or two seconds of silence, then shots crack around me. The BAR opens up to my right and still the little men in brown advance.

I have never had such an awful feeling of impending doom or dread. I start to return fire, wishing for that solid thump and feel of the 7.62 round flying out the end of a rife when all I have is the crack and gentle recoil of my .30 M1 carbine. I am catching glimpses in my peripheral vision of what is going on, all around me, men running and trying to find better firing positions. I am losing my hearing as I squeeze off round after round, slowing down now and aiming better until bullets start to smack in the ground around me. I look over my shoulder; the jungle is so close. In there, I will find safety. I know my capabilities. If I can get to that green, safe place, I will be okay. Then it is all over as a massive fireball envelops the far side of the village. The earth shakes. I feel an unnatural heat. People are yelling at me. Then I am grabbed by the shoulder, and we run for the safety of the green world I know.

* * *

The flight to Asia had taken almost eight hours, six hours of that flying time being in Australian airspace, or over Australia proper. It is, indeed, a massive island. There were very few people on board, and it was almost empty. I landed at Singapore airport, not knowing what to expect. I stood in the doorway; this one I would walk through not jump out of. The door opened. After the air conditioning and subtle light of the interior of the plane, the glare coming off the apron and the Singapore heat hit me like a blast furnace. After only a few steps, I was bathed in sweat, my clothes clinging to me. I cleared customs, leaving behind the air-conditioned comfort of the airport.

A put–put cab was waiting; Singapore was a pleasant place to start my journey. The wars were further north or north-east in another world. I moved to Bangkok to get my visa for Vietnam. I would not get to Vietnam. I was not the only person skulking around looking for work. In any war, there will always be someone trying to sell something, find something or someone. As the old saying goes, if you want to dance, you have got to be on the dance floor. The powers that be had made it clear that no regular US ground troops were to become involved in Laos, and they never did. A little-known fact is there was a large contingent of western soldiers operating all over the place, who came from who knows where. As I passed through Thailand, I would be given a knapsack for my worldly possession, a set of fatigues, a pair of boots, along with a .30 M1 carbine (acceptable deniability) and seven thirty-round magazines. The boots and pack I gave back. I had my own. People were travelling from other major centres around Asia into Saigon. The war in Vietnam only got to Saigon proper towards the end. The only armed US troops in Saigon were the Military Police, and the Marines at the US Embassy. Life carried on much as usual, similar to any other Asian city.

It all began to change after the Tet Offensive. Some knew of the war in Vietnam as the Second Indochina war or the American War, which started sometime in 1955 and included the old French Indochinese countries of Laos, Vietnam and Cambodia. Conflict in these countries was just an extension of what was called the Cold War. It was not the only war going on at that time. There were many in the grander scheme of things. It was not a 'big war' until it became what is today termed a media war.

I was 8 years old, and getting ready for my first sea trip to Africa when it all started. The war was to endure, even after the fall of Saigon in 1975, the same year I was first wounded when operating with the Special Air Service half a world away on the 14 March, two days before my birthday. The dates hold no significance. The American War became well known as it was the first media war. The conflicts in Africa went unheralded. Fighting for independence in South East Asia had been going since 1945, if not before. Covert operators were working all over Asia.

In 1968 the Tet Offensive took place; it was to be the bloodiest and most protracted battle fought in Vietnam. Although the Americans and South Vietnamese were able to defeat all the communist forces in time, the offensive unsettled the American people a great deal having been told that the communists were on the run, that there was a light at the end of the tunnel, and that they the communists had no capability for a large-scale offensive. The communists never won the Tet offensive; they were pushed back, and American troops retook every town overrun by them. In Hue, the bloodiest battle of all, the communists executed thousands of people before being defeated by the American ground forces, primarily the Marines. It did, however, cause the great American public to ask why they had been lied to, and, of course, governments always lie to their people. By the time I was in Laos, the Americans were back in control, and the war would carry on but things would never be the same.

Chang Mai is some 400 kilometres north of Bangkok; it had been recommended to me by an American serviceman I had met in a place called the Piano Bar just off some grubby little street. Thailand was awash with Americans on R&R, cold drinks that they call sodas, and Coca-Cola, and why would it not be as it was a sure sign of American imperialism. Chang Mai had a reputation for beautiful women, although its nightlife was not as boisterous as in Bangkok; in many regards, it was quite provincial. I stayed just off the Wichanon road in the Thai Pang Hotel. It was different, comfortable enough and was, for want of another word, a bordello or cat house, most of the rooms rented by working girls, some very beautiful and some not so much, but all very friendly and pleasant.

The offer was of an excellent job with an American company that had done a lot of work in this part of the world. I was to wait and meet my contact in a teahouse; the contact person, strangely enough, did not look like a Thai but was. At that time in South East Asia there was such a hotchpotch of regular and irregular forces it was like looking into a can of worms. Jimmy, that's the name he gave, although I had some doubt as to its authenticity. He was interested in everything, in a subtle, gentlemanly manner. He was interrogating me like any job interview. He was a linguist of note and spoke many languages. Did he have the authority to tell me stuff? You never know who or what a person is until they die. Or someone writes a book. He was a dichotomy. He had thick wavy hair, most unusual as Asian people have straight black hair. He sounded very American. I would later learn he was Thai by birth, but his parents and grandparents came from different countries. When I asked where, he would just wave in a general direction and say a small village I would not have heard of. I don't think he was indifferent to his origins, just that over the years he had been so many different people, never really knowing who he was. Or maybe he would rather not have me know. He did not interact well with others; our conversation was very one-sided. Who he was and where he came from remains a mystery. Guided to an office sometime later, Jimmy would simply disappear. I would never see him again. They, the elusive, unknown them or they, now wanted to know what experience I had, and about my military background. It is no secret if you're looking for soldiering work, to go to an area of conflict and talk to people. It's a bit more refined nowadays; one is contracted to a company, with offices in the UK or the USA and registered in Hong Kong or some obscure island, and there you have it. I have made more than one faux pas and been asked to leave by more than one embassy after speaking with the military attaché. I am a person of interest to some intelligence organizations. I made mistakes. I never had problems with the fact I had been in the Australian military; in some regards, it added to my prestige.

My life as a contractor could be summed up as shadowy at best at one end and at the other somewhat dubious, if not all the time then most times. It was and still is today a profession full of contradictions, inconsistencies and denial. I have signed documents such as the Official Secrets Act on more than one occasion and non-disclosure forms at others, not knowing what they meant or how long the elusive powers could keep them. Only being told you don't tell people who you are, where you have been and what you did. Apart from being honour bound with the possibility of never working again in my chosen profession, I have done just that. I now see British parachute soldiers, decorated American officers and contractor operators charged with murder thirty and even forty years later; it is not going to happen to me. Some of the penalties for breaching contracts are serious stuff when you're young, as some documents have no moratorium or statutes of limitation. Even today, I am not prepared to test whether this is fact or fiction. On more than one occasion, I would work and live with people who were patriotic, masters of their craft, good soldiers and intelligence operators who when trying to live in the real world would be of questionable character. I had willingly stepped through the looking glass and was now being interviewed by a mad hatter. I understood.

Thailand had a king that most people revered. They were royalists, nationalistic and militarized. They firmly believed in the domino theory and were the second-largest contributor of troops to the Vietnam War effort, after the US. When I told any Thai person I had been in the army, it was seen as normal; why would a man not want to defend his king and country? If soldiering was my bag and I was going to be on their side, the general view was that every little bit helped. The Thai people are gentle, they do not get drunk and batter one another, and, by and large, they are very respectful in both their speech and actions toward their fellow man, yet they were willing soldiers. They are not a warrior race such as the Nepalese Gurkha, but they volunteered in their droves when the Thai government sent them to Vietnam. Maybe because Thailand borders on Laos and Laos borders on China: now there is an incentive.

Later I signed documents to say I would not discuss with any party anything about anything. I asked if I could have a copy. They told me, 'No, you don't need one.' I did ask if I could have time to read it before signing, again being told, 'No, you don't need to, it's all basic stuff.' 'They' then went on to say that should I break the cardinal rule and reveal anything to anybody, they would simply deny it, or I would spend a long time in prison. One gentleman looked at my passport, turned to his partner and muttered it looked okay even if a little pristine. I wanted to ask what the job entailed. They, in turn, asked if I did drugs and for information about the Australian Army, my unit and my military number. Which I gave, as we were all on the same side, weren't we? But most of all they wanted to know why I was there. Another person came in and asked a different set of questions; I gave them more family information. They then gave me documents to fill in again. The fact that I don't do forms well was not helping the process along. I must have looked concerned so they occasionally told me everything was going to be just fine. And not to worry, it's only administration and being an old soldier, I would appreciate how 'our people' just love their copies of everything. 'It makes them feel secure.' They asked me to come back later. As I walked past an office, I distinctly heard two people talking, one a very Australian voice, and another with an English accent. The door slammed shut as I passed. I later rummaged in my gear to find additional photos I had taken in Bangkok for my visa to

Vietnam. The one I never used I kept as a souvenir. Two days later, as instructed, I went back. I had the job. I left for upcountry. My employment was dependent on removing all identification from my wardrobe, and my life.

Laos was a jumble of people; it was the proverbial melting pot. It had Americans who came from Germany, being neither American nor German. There were special forces, but not Americans: they had had to leave some time ago because of a treaty that called for the withdrawal of all foreign troops. So, who were the ones still working there? Laos was officially a civil war, not a war of independence but war is war, what's in a name. The place was a phantasmagoria. No one knew who was what. It had been running like that since the 1950s. No one in the real world had a clue. I think we on the ground were the same. At one airbase they had a movie house that showed dubbed moves. At the back was a raised area that was a separate room with an enormous glass window where people would sit and watch the film in English. I sat next to one person and, being a stranger in casual conversation, asked where he came from, and other usual pleasantries. He stuttered a reply that 'Uncle Sam don't like us to talk about that.' From the bad English, I knew he was American. Overweight for Special Forces but not too heavy to push buttons. When the movie started, he removed himself to the other side of the room.

From here on in I was a non-person; I no longer existed. I got an ID card with my photo saying I was a researcher for an NGO that did studies and observation. What I was meant to research or study I have no idea. It was simple: the money was good and in cash.

I went by air transport to a forward base; I still had not been told my line function. The last time I asked the reply was, 'You're a soldier, right?'

'Yes.'

'There ya go.'

They did just as they pleased. By then, I was on a rotary-wing. I was to meet my point of contact only five times, with meetings in Chang Mai, Vientiane in Laos and the last time in Bangkok. The documents they gave said very little at all, but it was a good photo; they took it back off me when I left. We sat and talked. I gave the answers I thought they wanted. My new contact sat forward in the chair, looked at me and said, 'Your line function is going to be somewhat different to what you have been told.' I was about to interject but didn't. He went into some operational detail knowing full well they had me and I was not going anywhere as they owned all the means of transport. I went back to our compound outside the base at the end of the runway. I lay on my bed that night, listening to jets taking off using their afterburners; they must be fully loaded. I never heard them return. I played with my new toy, the .30 M1 carbine; it is basic and straightforward. I had never handled one before and was fascinated by it. I was later issued rounds for it – they are FMJ and come in a teeny-weeny packet. The bullets looked frightfully small compared to the Australian 7.62 self-loading rifle. Another teeny-weenie object, a radio, was then given to me. If Celeste had seen it, she would have called it quaint. In the 1960s there was no war in a faraway land called Laos.

We had done a visual recce on the ambush site: it was where two tracks converged and offered an excellent killing ground. The Big American was right: my line function had changed. I could view the track as it came up the slow elevation from the south along the side of the hill, the other track coming up from the south-western side. We were a reconnaissance patrol but the temptation to ambush was too great for the people I was with. Most had suffered personal loss at the hands of the communists; they didn't like them. They were very aggressive. At the top of the elevation, the tracks formed a cross, almost like the top of a hot cross bun, then dropped down out of sight some fifty to a hundred metres away. I glassed the area with my binoculars; it looked as if whoever was going to use the track would stop for a rest after the climb. Did I know this for a fact? No, but I had been around soldiers long enough to know this was a natural resting place for a swig of water and a smoke. If they stopped long enough, maybe they would put in all-round defence. I was counting on the fact each one would be thinking they owned the whole country and would do what all troops other than SF troops do: they would drop their packs, plonk down on their bums and rest. I had been told and accepted that if I was caught, the people I was fighting could be very cruel. But as good as they were, I had seen them 'run' with no legs, just stumps, to get away, having been shot or blown up. They didn't want to die either. The problem was if I ambushed on the junction, I had four directions to watch. I opted to move to the northern side and ambush on one track coming from the north. I checked what was the easiest climb and then placed my team on the top of it, what I thought would be the approach. An ambush is not an exact science; you work with what you have. I chose the natural, northern side because I know soldiers, and most of the shit was coming down from the north anyway. I lay next to the BAR and then we waited and waited and waited.

The ambush was sprung late afternoon. There is not much to tell. When done right these things are almost like an exercise. Life ends quickly, or it should, in a good ambush. They went down very fast; there was a feeble attempt to respond but no flanking movement. One of the enemy went back and sat down on his bum. I must have hit him half a dozen times but he would not roll over dead. I know I was hitting him. My ears were ringing. I could not hear the strikes, but I could see them. My last shot was a headshot and still he never went down. I put in stop firing and we waited. We should have bugged out, but it was late afternoon and I knew darkness would hide us in an hour; we would be well in jungle cover by then. I went over to my reluctant corpse. He had gone down but his pack had rested up against a small rock which caused to sit him upright. Had

I been using a 7.62 elephant gun, it would have knocked him off his feet with the first shot. Strange things happen with ballistics.

We grabbed the enemy packs and weapons and descended into the safety of darkness. We rested up. I thought I was going mad as I heard trucks all night long. Who drives vehicles through the jungle, especially at night? I thought about taking a bearing on the transport noise and calling in an airstrike but it was too late so I didn't. I had the troops move then move some more. We did a 180-degree dogleg back on our tracks to ensure we weren't being followed. Then we slept.

I had stepped through that magic mirror and found the Mad Hatter, the Cheshire Cat and all. I was to discover I was good at ambushing and intelligence-gathering. Later I would forget the name and coordinates of every place I went and everything I did or saw.

I took over a small protected compound on a hillside; most people have the idea that South East Asia is all jungle and swamp, but you can find places with slow, undulating hills that look very much like the Highlands of Scotland, and rock formations that are similar to the Nyanga Mountains in Rhodesia (Zimbabwe). I had been a non-person for some time now. Should any white people, westerners that is, on the off-chance visit or try and talk to me, I was told I was to run away. Extreme measures would have to be taken if I did not, to sort it out, to clean up the situation. In normal circumstances, extreme would mean getting fired, no job, no money. I was 21 years old on my first contract and I had already seen the extreme measures they could take. I never spoke to anyone ever, not even when I was on R&R in Vientiane. What they, whoever they were, had started as a hearts and minds programme had now mutated in a short time. It was an intelligence operation that was fast turning into an organization that was gaining the capability to wage war. They were doing just what they liked and getting away with it. I was that wearied kid who never spoke to anyone, ever. They had no end of people they wanted to kill. The killing part was not the problem; it was trekking all of God's green earth trying to find the right ones to kill. I did my job and was good at it. I still don't know how it worked; it just did. It may be hard to believe and even harder to understand and to some tasteless, but I was having the time of my life and being paid for it.

Laos was not journalist-friendly; the infrastructure at best was abysmal, other than the Ho Chi Minh Trail that was a bloody great highway, in places being twenty-five feet wide. The communists controlled two-thirds of the country; it was hazardous all right, as no one would bring your body back if you were killed or captured. The best way to get around was to know someone, who knew someone who had a helicopter: this, would, of course, present problems, as they did not exist. Even if some of the airbases in Laos were enormous complexes, officially they were not there, so could not be found or used, meaning the journalists stayed in Vientiane and drank. How do your report on things that never happened? Besides, no one was saying, 'Hey buddy, give you a ride to the front?' as no one knew where the front was, either in the lowlands or in the mountains where no journalist could get to. And why would anyone want to go there anyway?

Our civic action started in November 1968 and, going into early December, we did a lot of recon work that went on for weeks. We called in a lot of T-28s after locating anything that looked like it should not be there. The government was generally reticent about reacting to any contact. I had been brought back across the Mekong to work among the local tribes to counter the communist encroachment in Phetchabun, a province in north-central Thailand. The communists, many of whom were related to villagers that side of the Mekong, had moved down across from Laos and infiltrated that remote area. There was evidence that they had started to entrench themselves some time ago. This whole thing stemmed from neglect. The Thai nationals in the urban centres were far more sophisticated than the

Early days before the wheels came off. The term 'an agreeable early childhood' would be an apt description of my early life.

Vehicle loaded with our out-of-Africa tent, on safari to Portuguese East Africa (Mozambique).

Returning to England by ship. 1960s family photo of Mum, Dad, Keith, Sharon and me.

Walking-out dress after completion of basic parachute course at RAAF parachute training school, Fort Gellibrand, Williamstown, New South Wales, Australia.

Kitted up outside the training hangar waiting for first 'lob' (parachute descent) from the ramp exit of a Caribou.

Me wearing cobble-wobbly boots – good for climbing, but maybe not the best for the rain and mud of South East Asia.

Elizabeth and Guy, my only child – my Australian family. The odds were against her right from the start. Life might have been different had I not messed up.

Small raids course, next to old Second World War canoes. We later progressed to Klepper canoes, much lighter and faster.

The Vietnam War was fought across ill-defined borders, one big playground for alphabet soup intelligence agencies. The cutting is the only thing I came out with.

Our life vests were pilots' Mae Wests, seen here inflated. Mae West had some interesting proportions.

Me abseiling and climbing. We had our share of fatalities.

345 Platoon recruit course passing-out parade and order of march. I was posted to 2 Para – 2nd Battalion The British Parachute Regiment – in time for Northern Ireland.

DEPOT THE PARACHUTE REGIMENT
and AIRBORNE FORCES

Passing-Out Day

for

345 Platoon

Reviewing Officer :
Wing-Commander R. D. Mullins, AFC
Late Commanding Officer,
No. 1 Parachute Training School

5TH DECEMBER, 1969

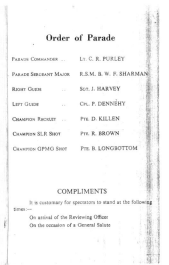

Order of Parade

PARADE COMMANDER	LT. C. R. PURLEY
PARADE SERGEANT MAJOR	R.S.M. B. W. F. SHARMAN
RIGHT GUIDE	SGT. J. HARVEY
LEFT GUIDE	CPL. P. DENNEHY
CHAMPION RECRUIT	PTE. D. KILLEN
CHAMPION SLR SHOT	PTE. R. BROWN
CHAMPION GPMG SHOT	PTE. B. LONGBOTTOM

COMPLIMENTS

It is customary for spectators to stand at the following times:—

On arrival of the Reviewing Officer
On the occasion of a General Salute

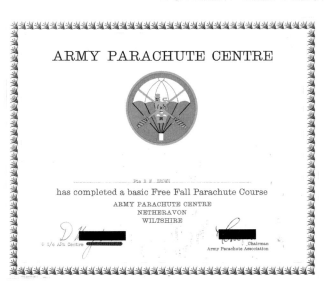

ARMY PARACHUTE CENTRE

Pte R W BROWN

has completed a basic Free Fall Parachute Course

ARMY PARACHUTE CENTRE
NETHERAVON
WILTSHIRE

O I/c APA Centre

Chairman
Army Parachute Association

Freefall certificate, 1971. Having done freefall in Northern Ireland, I could say I'd lobbed freefall into an operational area – but that would be stretching it.

When doing roadblocks or cordon and search, a 'sharpshooter' would be placed on high ground or rooftops to cover the search teams who would occasionally find some excellent pieces, real collector's items.

She was crying and all she kept on saying was, 'Dear God, dear God soldier, don't let them kill us.'

On the second tour, the battalion split down to section strength at different locations. My section took up residence in an old house at a T-junction. The house was later razed to the ground in a bomb explosion.

Northern Ireland at the end of my first tour, 1970. We had just got the old mill sorted out and now it was time to hand over to another regiment.

I learned to freefall out of an old 1930s de Havilland Rapide biplane. Apparently, RAF fighter pilots would put in for leave so they could fly this stringbag.

My first three-second delay – freefall. Everyone has to start somewhere.

The de Havilland Rapide was a wonderful old plane to freefall from; you always came out stable. Our delay time was now getting longer.

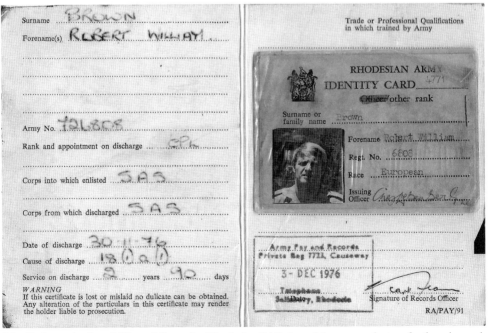

My service book from the British Parachute Regiment.

My discharge book and ID card from the Rhodesian SAS. I would go on to do two further six-week call-ups. On 21 December 1979, a ceasefire was declared and the war was over.

I am sitting with my back resting against my Bergen, some low foliage supporting it. I watch two young SAS troops trying to get a body into a large plastic bag.

Me and the Golf team, Iraq, 2004/5. I completed four separate Special Forces selections and soldiered in four different armies. Later I operated as a civilian soldier working on contract in Sudan and Iraq

From left: Me, Bob (Brit Para), John (Australian SAS) and Ian (Royal Marine Commando) who was KIA. Waiting for deployment forward – with clean boots.

Teams would change, to gain experience working with other personnel with different skills levels.

On the way home – extraction by chopper after a camp attack in 'Porkers' (Mozambique), with the face veil that almost got me shot in the head.

Camp attacks into Mozambique. The Cyclone 7 Alouette trooper could take only four fully equipped SAS troops. Choppers would dummy-land three or four times before we deplaned some miles from the target camp, then we walked in for the attack at first light.

Coming back to firm base, then reissue and redeploy.

My first ambush site in Mozambique. The ambush commander was Sgt Frank V, the team Bates M and Joe B, later KIA Iraq in the early 2000s.

Classic ambush site in 'Porkers' (Mozambique). I was taught by the Australians never to walk on tracks or trails, a lesson well learnt, but obviously not by others.

Scotty Baby (USMC, RLI and SAS) with a thousand-yard stare after an all-day running contact. When working internally (in Rhodesia) we used standard issue equipment and uniforms. 'Rob, I am so fucked, I can't remember: did I just get out of that chopper or am I meant to be getting back into it?'

Deployment by chopper, always pointing north. No one would know where we had deplaned.

ID cards.

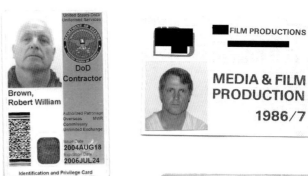

Prepping irregulars for the coming storm. Covert training, Zululand, Natal, 1994.

Our first covert instructor course. I could instruct five or ten would-be dissidents. If I trained them to be instructors, I would be instructing a massively compounded number.

Lectures and training NGOs, infiltration of the Christian Church.

Zambian detention order, a simple bit of poor-quality paper that could have cost me ten to twenty years in prison or even death and a shallow grave.

Revocation of Zambian detention order.

Firearms training for female NGO personnel.

Somewhere in Angola.

Me, location unknown, with an R4 rifle.

Once more, I found myself with an intelligence organization able to wage war.

In this case, staying off roads and tracks would apply – an ideal area for a deliberate ambush.

Barbara on one of her better days, but she would soon relapse back into depression.

Home away from home. Life is what you make it at a covert bush training camp.

Me (right) with Doug, a man with an attitude deluxe but who turns up when you need him.

Somewhere north of South Africa. Sometimes you have to work with what you have: 12.7 rounds with rusty belts and unstable bombs, but do they work?

Early morning cold-clearing a patrol training base.

The most photographed gun in Iraq, if not the world, the .50 Browning.

Me and my gun team of 6-foot-plus Fijians. Having served in Rhodesia and South Africa, I had fewer problems and no kickbacks from any of these fine people.

The firefight had just started when down the street came the Strykers … all guns blazing. Now, what was the chance of that?

Iraq – staying off roads and tracks in this case would probably not apply.

I first worked with Gurkha troops then later with Fijians – no problems with any of them. A a soldier is a soldier and a friend if he's shooting in the same direction as you.

Setting head space for the .50 Browning.

The A10 went *brrrrrrrrrrr* … don't piss off the Americans.

Me in winter kit looking like the Michelin man.
Winter in Iraq is sunny at times but very, very cold.

Certificate of commendation
giving operational achievements.

TASK FORCE FREEDOM

MOSUL, IRAQ

Certificate of Appreciation

Presented to

ROBERT BROWN

Shooter

For your dedication and support to Task Force Freedom during Operation Iraqi Freedom III. Your outstanding performance and attention to detail have contributed greatly to the overall success of the command's mission. Your actions and example should be emulated by all and reflect great credit upon yourself, Task Force Freedom and the people of Iraq.

Given this 26ᵗʰ day of March 2005
In Mosul, Iraq

KEVIN J. BERGNER
BG, USA
Commanding General

DEPARTMENT OF THE ARMY
Headquarters, Task Force Freedom
Multinational Brigade-Northwest (MNB-NW), Mosul, Iraq
APO AE 09385

REPLY TO
ATTENTION OF:

CIBI-CG 28 March 2005

MEMORANDUM FOR: Mr. Charlie Andrews, President and CEO, Global Risk Strategies, Ltd., London, England.

SUBJECT: Letter of Commendation for Mr. Robert Brown, Global Risk Strategies Ltd.

Mr. Robert Brown performed his duties as a Security Consultant on the project known as Operation Northstar in an exemplary manner. Operation Northstar's mission was to provide Humanitarian support from March 2004 to April 2005 in the Northern provinces of Iraq. His significant contributions were instrumental to the overall successes achieved by Global towards that endeavor.

During his tenure, Mr. Robert Brown participated in numerous Humanitarian Convoy protection missions ranging from the escorting of fuel, gravel, force protection barriers, general cargo and personnel. Additionally, Mr. Brown assisted the Task Force during Iraq's first historic democratic election. In his capacity he was involved in the static security and personnel security of Election Staff Officials located at various locations in Mosul. His efforts and those of the Global Team facilitated a safe, orderly and responsive security cell helping the election process.

In addition, Mr. Brown was also significantly involved in the Route Reconnaissance/Security of main travel arteries and supply routes enabling Humanitarian Support missions to traverse freely, safely and unimpeded through and around Mosul, Iraq in direct support of the United States Army Task Force Freedom. In the performance of those tasks, the Global team safely deactivated numerous improvised explosive devices (IED) and was involved in numerous combative engagements.

Of note are missions that require mentioning, specifically the involvement of Personal Security Detachment (PSD) for escort of scientists involved in the uncovering of war atrocities against Saddam Hussein' at the mass gravesites near the Al Hatr ruins. Those same PSD duties were also applied to the senior Coalition Provisional Authority representative, Herro Mustafa and the Governors of Mosul Liaison Officer. No casualties were involved during this two-month assignment.

Mr. Brown's efforts have contributed significantly to the development of a more secure Iraq. His performance reflects great credit on himself and Global Risk Strategies, Ltd.

PETER C. BAYER, JR.
COL, AR
Chief of Staff

From the US Chief of Staff, a letter
of commendation giving line function
and operational achievements.

South of Mosul, Iraq.

Mosul, Iraq. Soldiering can
be fun, but when it's bad,
it's very very bad.

Me at FOB Freedom, 2004/5.

Iraq. Call signs One Alpha and Four Alpha – teams would change daily, as who went to which call sign was very much a case of office politics.

If we had to self-recover, a call sign could be out on the road for up to twenty-six hours.

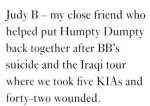

Judy B – my close friend who helped put Humpty Dumpty back together after BB's suicide and the Iraqi tour where we took five KIAs and forty-two wounded.

hill tribe people, whom I would call more aboriginal with a strong strain of Chinese genetics. For many years they had been ignored. Some Thai nationals thought they were not really even Thai. It was an ideal breeding ground for insurgents to work in.

My interpreter finds a new track to an old village. It leads from a main road back into the jungle, then into what is a deserted area. Do I want to go in there? Not really, but it's my job. I move a hundred metres parallel to the road, keeping it on my right-hand side, but staying two or three metres off the road proper, close enough to the jungle edge should I have to take cover. I don't like walking down tracks, trails or streets. I will do a dogleg to my left flank and come into the village from the opposite side of the track. We are in an area of low scrub. My people go to ground; some of the more experienced start to put in an all-round defence. I pass the word down not to bother – we are going in, although I am convinced no one will be there as the Jolly Green – a Sikorsky HH-3E helicopter – had been flying around all day. We are ready for a basic camp attack but will there be anyone at home? I hear cooking pots clatter – they have either fallen off someone's pack, or they are busy cooking. We go in hard, yelling. We are in open ground in a deserted village with no cover. We come under heavy fire from the jungle edge – we have caught them at mealtime. All around me men are running. I catch glimpses of what is going on, shouts drowned by RPG rockets. Somchai is on my right. I hear the slow automatic fire of his weapon, an old grease gun; he yells at me to run, run quickly which is advice I don't need as I am already doing just that. At least everyone is going in the same direction. As soon as we hit the jungle edge on the other side of the village, I am yelling to our people that they must turn and wheel back through and not chase whoever, as they could end up in an ambush. Somchai knows what I want: we have been together for two months. Now the young officer is shouting, trying to wheel the men. I sit on the ground gasping for air; someone comes to see if I am okay and not hurt; I am breathing so hard they think I have been wounded. Already they are starting to put in a defence perimeter. I am completely shattered, exhausted. Somchai stays with me. I am okay. My M1 is hot as I pick it up to move. I am surprised I have only used one and a half magazines. It is getting dark now. We must move as we hear a Jolly Green coming back and it may mistakenly open fire on us. We have no communications as my teeny-weeny radio is not working. We move out. I am absolutely, irretrievably fucked as this is the first camp attack and advance to contact I have done. I make a mental note that from here on in I am a reconnaissance and ambush kind of guy, not infantry.

We had one of our meetings at the end of March 1969 and talked as usual, only this time, it was a little different. He went on about how things would be changing that year. I got the feeling he was trying to say something but finding it hard, like 'Rob, it's coming to an end. Uncle Sam has made some changes at the top, political stuff way above my pay grade, and a lot of what we do is not meant to be happening.' We were being marginalized as new and better things were coming. Electronic warfare was not long off now and there would be no more use for our kind of intelligence systems, boots on the ground. I don't think I was disappointed as much as tired. Too tired to fight or object, maybe it was time to go. I had earned and learned a lot in the time I had been there. I had not lost anyone, and I was coming out with all my fingers and toes. I thought, let it go, Rob, so I made it easy for him.

'Okay, when must I be out?'

'Be ready to move in a week down to Bangkok then to any place you want on the ticket.'

I think he was wondering about all those new administration types coming in and whether he would keep his job. When I finally came out, the first western song I heard was by the Beatles called 'Hey Jude'. I wasn't back in the real world yet, but it was a start. I completed my contract.

Mid-1969 found me miles away from Laos, Thailand and warm weather. I had come back to Western Europe. Everywhere I went now felt flat. I was thinking of going back, but it's not the kind of thing you leave and return to. You are ever there, or you are not. Strange occurrences and ideas used to pop into my mind: the sound of a launch, that unique *plop* sound of the small blast of propellant when a bomb drops down a mortar tube. I was sitting on a London tube train; I had forgotten where I was going and was hoping I would remember before I passed my stop. I almost unexpectedly turned to a young girl next to me to tell her that when an aeroplane drops its ordnance, even if you're a kilometre away, the ground shakes under you and if closer you can feel the heat. If I could remember where I was going, I could have asked her if I was on the right line. I wanted someone to talk to without sounding crazy stupid. I didn't have anyone, so I screwed the lid on tight. I got off at the next stop. I was thinking of ways to get back to Australia as I walked and gazed nonchalantly in shop windows. I found myself in front of a British Army recruiting office. I thought of 2 Commando, Laos, jungle nights, river crossings and helicopter rides, along with all sorts of dumb things before a Lewis Carroll line from years ago came into my head: *if it was so, it might be; and if it were so, it would be; but as it isn't, it ain't. That's logic.*

To this day, I am still trying to understand just what does it all mean. I pushed the door open and went into the warmth of the army recruiting office; maybe I would get a cup of tea: the Brits were good at that.

Chapter 4

The UK and Northern Ireland

Then it's Tommy this, an' Tommy that, an' 'Tommy, 'ow's yer soul?'
But it's 'Thin red line of 'eroes' when the drums begin to roll.

Rudyard Kipling, 'Tommy'

If there is one thing that you can rely on in the UK, it has to be the weather; here I was in London in the middle of the year and it was cold, or maybe I had not got acclimatized, being out of the Far East for only a short a time. I pushed the door open and entered the British Army Recruiting Office. One lone soldier staffed it; obviously, business was slow – this was a one-man operation. The one man, a sergeant, was a little bit roly poly, but he did have some ribbons on his dress uniform, so he must have been somewhere at some time and done something. Of course, this must have been when he was in better shape. I must have been the first customer of the day; he greeted me with a cheerful 'Good morning, sir.' Troops learn very quickly; everyone is a Sir until proven otherwise. If you're unsure, salute it and if it's standing still, paint it.

'What can we do for you today, sir? Or where would you like us to send you? My little personal joke.' He seemed quite pleasant.

I played dumb and asked him about the medals he had and what they were or represented. He explained where and when he got them; the man had done much soldering. Recruiting offices must be where the British put old soldiers out to pasture. It was early; maybe business would pick up later I wondered if he had a quota to fill. I informed him I wasn't interested in the army but had come in out of curiosity. I did get a second cup of tea; he had biscuits as well so we chatted some more. They had just brought in a new pilot scheme; he explained many of the young people today had never been away from their mother for more than a day and this was when they went to watch an away football match. He then continued that one does not just sign on to join the army. No! One goes away to an army camp for a week or ten days. You get paid for the week, and they show you what it's like in the modern army and they show you all the things you can do. Just a paid holiday really and if it's not your thing, you go home.

'You sound as if you're from Australia, by the way. What are you doing for the next week or two? If you're curious you can do the week; then you will have something to tell the folks back home in Oz.' The Brits always pronounce Australia with an Ou as in Ouz-stralia. 'I'll make out a travel warrant. Do you have much to pack, Rob?' (We were now one first name terms – the third cup of tea.) 'You're going to enjoy the week.' He tore out the travel warrant and handed it to me; it was for the next day. Strangely enough, I took it.

The train ride did not take me to the other side of the world, as previous train rides had. I arrived at my destination: there was a military bus waiting for me, and nine young men, some very young, with small bags. None of us had packed for an extended stay. I surmised everyone was there for the week's money. It was a proper army base. I can't recall the name but it was a short distance outside of London. Another roly-poly sergeant welcomed us, a pleasant fellow that everyone must have liked as they all referred to him as Tom. If the ten of us had wobbled, we would have looked like a row of ducks, mother duck up front with her ten little ducklings following. A uniform, which strangely enough did fit, was issued to us – just a shirt and trousers, along with some bedding but no hat and no insignia or badges. We kept our footwear. Tom then escorted us to our quarters that were to be our home for a week. It was now lunchtime, and that meant food. Now, asked to give an opinion and critique on the fare, in truth, it was not bad. Mind you, I had been living in a jungle village for a time, so I suppose my expectations when it came to food was not very high. Everyone agreed, some expressing it was better than they got at home. We were walked around and shown the NAAFI (Navy Army Air Force Institute), an essential part of any Trog's life, the equivalent of what I knew as the American PX.

I enlisted in the British Army on 11 June 1969 and went straight to Aldershot in Hampshire to the depot of The Parachute Regiment, as a recruit. I did not inform them I was a trained or seasoned parachute soldier or special forces-trained. I saw no benefit in doing so. I was looking for a place to rest; I kept out of the way, shut my mouth and soldiered without attracting too much attention to myself. Although, after a few weeks, the training staff did notice that things came relatively easy to me.

It was self-evident that army recruiting officers and staff from all other units attempted to dissuade every person who wanted to join the Parachute Regiment from doing so, including older or long-term parachute soldiers themselves, as well NCOs whose job it was to conduct the necessary training of such. In the first instance, all the aspirational applicants were encouraged to leave there and then, to save the embarrassment of failing in their pathetic efforts to become remotely like them, the para instructors. From day one, they didn't want any of us to join their regiment. This attitude was made clear by restricting the entry of recruits who tried to get into the regiment by wearing them out and grinding them down. The hardened instructors were doing all they could to inflict pain and suffering on the many wannabes, as they went through basic training up to P Company. Every couple of weeks, we would have the separation of the goats from the sheep. Nothing too formal, sometimes before we all went on a run, Sergeant Harvey alias Bunny would point and say, 'You and you, over that side of the room' and when the little group was large enough, he would tell the rest of us, 'You lot outside' and when we came back from the run, the you and yous had gone.

Basic training was what it was: hard painful, wet and muddy, much the same as all training for parachute soldiers with that little extra thrown in by the Brits, varying levels of discomfort and savagery, inflicted on would-be airborne warriors all over the English-speaking world. Instructors who had killed and maimed an enemy in the past, now pushing new troops to the edge of extinction. P Company instructors work on a reverse commission: the instructor who has the least recruits functioning or in working order at the end of this selection process wins. We lesser mortals spent hours running across tank tracks in a vast, unforgiving location, which had been ploughed by tracked vehicles. It had furrows, ditches and trenches that a recruit could disappear into under the weight of the ever-present log or telephone pole. This appendage was grafted on to each one of us when we first started P Company. Tanks and other tracked vehicles would churn up the ground under adverse conditions. The furrows that the tanks cut in the mud could be shallow to impossibly deep but always full of water. The impassable cuts left by the tracks were full of thick mud. We ran across, through or around and into the troughs of unbearably cold water, in freezing weather, and in the endless, omnipresent rain. (Or it was as dry as a desert, and the tracks of the tanks churned the ground into a fine powdery dust that you breathed in, coating your equipment and body, so all the recruits were of a uniform colour with bloodshot eyes glassed and vacant peering out of dust-caked faces. There was no moderate in-between on P Company.) Mainly, when selection started, a rain cloud hovered over the tank tracks. Copious amounts of icy water poured down onto the recruits for the duration. The tracked vehicles would mix and churn up heaps of soft, gooey, sludgy mud by the ton. After running through this slimy treacle-like substance, one's boots gained a good two kilograms in weight. This gummy substance stuck to your clothes and your body, and if you fell over it coated the large, heavy steel-pot helmet you wore, adding more weight. Mud sticks to everything like a quality adhesive. It gets in your eyes and inside your clothes and over the top of your boots. It becomes an abrasive, rubbing and chafing joints and skin in the most delicate parts of your anatomy. All this suffering accompanied you and your team, six men and the pole. The pole was a cumbersome, massive wooden telegraph pole, which you ran with everywhere. It was issued at the start of P Company with a uniform entirely different from standard-issue attire, and might include a red, blue or even green sweatshirt and green jungle pants.

You will parade the next morning, clean-shaved with said uniform washed clean and pressed. Ready to be coated in whatever again. The only thing you can't polish is your boots, but all the clay has to be removed from the treads. Your combat boots remain wet for the entire P Company. If you go to the laundromat in Aldershot any time between nightfall and one in the morning you will see large groups of zombie-like people washing the one set of this uniform they have, and trying to dry it. The platoon iron is back at camp, so once the clothes are clean and dry, the zombies return to their barrack rooms and stand in line to use the troop iron and ironing board. Your clothing is now fresh-pressed and ready for the morning mud run. Your only decision at this time is will you sleep standing up, so you don't have to 're-box' the bed, or lie down on the floor for a short time before the parade.

Selection once completed and, if still alive, I am off to RAF Abingdon to jump out of a British aircraft. Unlike the parachute course in Australia, the Brits do their first jump out of a balloon. I suppose it has something to do with costs. These massive blimps do not have motors or wings and things, and they don't need runways to take off from. They go up and down on the end of a cable. When empty they are winched down and loaded with the next chalk, or group of parachute soldiers, now in line waiting to jump. Jumping from a balloon is very different from when you exit a plane. The slipstream from an aircraft carries you along and down until your parachute deploys; with the balloon jump there is no slipstream: it's a dead drop straight down, much the same as jumping off a very tall building. The gondola swings even at ground level, as it hangs below the balloon. As you gain height, it seems as if the basket takes on a life of its own, the pitching and swinging become more pronounced. The opening that you will exit from is just that – a small aperture in the side of the basket. As you start to ascend, the aperture appears to grow in size. It starts to look just a little larger as you gain height, so you move further back, trying to get away from it. Once you're at 500 feet, this hole in the basket that is holding three or four other nervous bodies has taken on a much larger dimension. Everyone adjusts his stance, moving away in an effort not to fall out accidentally as the opening appears to be enormous. An extraordinary psychological reaction, because in about three minutes you're going to be standing with your toes almost over the edge of the gondola ready to jump out the very aperture you are trying to stay away from. The order comes to hook up, check equipment and count off. You are trying not to look down as you wait for the word go. There is no mechanical noise like from an aeroplane; just the soft sway of the gondola as feet shuffle around, no slipstream coming through the door and down past the chalk. No throb of engines, only you and the long straight drop down that will go on forever until you hit the ground if the 'chute does not open. Your height now is very high; you try and look professional. The PJI (parachute jump instructor) has a smile, or is it a smirk, on his face; he then looks sad, shaking his head as you stand in the door. What does he know that you don't? He shouts 'Go!' And you do; your body goes straight down; your stomach, and internal organs remain in the basket and take some time to catch up to the rest of you as you plummet towards the earth, You are out, and you drop like a stone and downnnnn you go then. Then *pop*, the parachute opens. Or it should. You look up and there it is, and that's the first 'lob' or jump you do on your way to becoming a Brit Para.

Having jumped and qualified with the Australians in 2 Commando, the ballooning up in an open cage and that dead drop does get the heart rate up. It's the first jump with the Brit Paras that everyone does, well almost everyone; they do get the occasional person who says no thank you, so they unhook him and sit him down and he goes somewhere and you never see him again. (One colleague on his first jump went down somewhat faster than usual when his parachute had a malfunction on his first descent. He flew his reserve just in time. Scared the be-jiminy out of the training staff, so much so, that on landing, the PJI put his arm around Doug's shoulder and, pointing to the gate that leads out into the real world, told him, 'Son, if I were you I would walk through that fucking gate and never come back again.' He never did walk away, but spends a lot of time, even after forty years, going to doctors' clinics and even the hospital, spending his disability pension on transport trying to sort out the back pain.)

Other than finding balloon jumps a strange and new experience, I found the commissioned officers in the British Army even more so. They are somewhat bemusing if not altogether unusual. I think it was a German general who once said the British soldier 'is a fearless lion, led by donkeys'. I found the British officer somewhat lacking when measured against the Australians. I don't mean the training is left wanting, as the British Paras are among the best of the best. I think weird is an appropriate word in their case. I believe the British subaltern is incubated on a faraway planet way out of sight of real people, a place where he can do very little damage either to himself or others. On this distant planet in an embryonic state he is programmed with the misconception that he knows everything, has tremendous power and a right to be obeyed regardless of outcome or consequences. Moreover, everyone has to do what he wants, or he will throw his toys out the cot. On completion of incubation, he is somehow mysteriously returned to the real world to appear in a company or battalion as a Rupert. He stands in front of unfortunate Trogs who also don't know where he has been or where he came from. The Sandhurst subaltern makes such stupid statements as 'I am the same as you chaps, you know, only I have spent three years at Sandhurst.' Alternatively, 'I have never been shot, but an air rifle did hit me once, and I can tell you it jolly well hurts.' I should imagine it jolly well would. 'So be careful where you shoot.' If lucky and by the grace of God, this nincompoop will partner with a seasoned veteran called a sergeant. If this is the case, many of the Trogs will live to become like the sergeant, mature and experienced. One will from time to time see said sergeant stroll away shaking his head and looking up to the stars, as if looking for divine guidance, or for some extraterrestrial vehicle that will beam our subaltern back up whence he came.

The first job of the sergeant is to find something for the new officer to do. This task must not be too complicated or dangerous and must not entail any cockamamie ideas thought up by an ideas man at Army HQ or from Sandhurst. That has nothing to do with anything at all. Just bring something for the Trogs to do so they don't get bored. A little something to keep them busy, give them something to do so they won't break things or wander off. I along with a platoon of parachute soldiers once dug holes in the ground to crawl into, then spent three futile days sitting in said holes. To this day, I still have no idea what it was about; they called the holes hides. With heat-seeking cameras that can pick up newly turned earth, what on earth were they thinking of, apart from keeping us busy? The best bet is to get Rupert to make tea; they are good at that, so I have been told. The sergeant's primary job is to keep the troops alive so they can do their job, which is to find the enemy and then kill him. The officer's job is to make sure all the administration is correct as he can go to jail for his administrative mistakes. The military gets given stacks of costly equipment that he, the new officer being at the bottom of the food chain, must sign for on a WOCS list. Then he hands the item to some Trog who in all probability will lose it or he becomes so personally attached to the expensive item that he thinks it is his and will want to keep it forever, cocking up the young officer's equipment list until he finds the Trog and gets it back. He will try to convince the troop to return the item as it was not given him for keeps. He will fail in this task of retrieving the object as the soldier will have forgotten where he put it, until the sergeant talks to him in a loving tone and convinces the Trog that giving it back would be the right thing to do. On arrival, he, the new and young subaltern, is told that his tactical mistakes (dead soldiers) can be buried. His administrative errors, if too frequent, will interrupt his climb to fame and higher office, and maybe even bring about his incarceration. With his tactical misadventures then generally buried, hidden below ground, if the numbers are acceptable losses, merely a lot, with a great deal of pomp he gets a medal, and if it's lots and lots, he receives a knighthood. He then resigns and goes into politics or the City to work in a bank that belongs to a distant family member or someone who happens to have been in such and such regiment in the days when horses and tight white riding breeches were in fashion. He will break bread from time to time with another someone, usually called Rodney or just a jolly good chap who also has a distinctly plummy accent.

I recall a briefing for a night drop, our instructions from Jet Jungle, a name give not because of his prowess as a jungle fighter but due to the fact he is green and dense.

'A Section will assemble on the red light, B on the green and HQ Section will assemble with me on the black light.'

The sergeant then goes to great pains to explain that stores do not have lights with black lenses as experience has shown 'they don't work well at night, sir'.

Then there was an incident; a bomb went off in Northern Ireland, one of many. Said, subaltern, after the bomb blast, leaps out of the vehicle, brandishing a pistol above his head shouting, 'Follow me chaps.' He charges up the main street in Belfast, with four Trogs not knowing exactly what he or they should charge. Prudence and experience dictating, they take cover and watch and shoot or wait for a secondary explosion. I put most of this down to inbreeding. Inbreeding results in the procreation of total imbeciles. Most of them either end up in the House of Lords or with commissions in the military, frequently the Guards or the Household Cavalry, commonly referred to as the Donkey Wallopers. Now and then one will slip through the cracks and ends up being normal; this is the basis of all Trogs' prayers, hopes and dreams: being blessed with a reasonable officer. Should they be that lucky and find him, Trogs will do their best. They will win battles for him, follow him over cliffs and through jungles. He will win medals for all their endeavours. When he leaves to accomplish greater things, he will be missed and remembered, with words such as 'He were all right, not too bad for a bloody Rupert. Let's hope we get another one like him', and sometimes, 'We could never be that lucky twice.' Many Ruperts are confused as to their value, worth and importance until taken under the wing of a rational-thinking and benevolent NCO who will keep him out of trouble, thereby saving not only his life but the lives of the troops, and helping said Rupert up the ladder of promotion and posted to a new job. Or better still to get him to that time of life where eventually he realizes that he too can die, as the other side don't use BB guns or air rifles. There is nothing special about him at all, other than the men who surround him. As one seasoned sergeant from the Welsh Guards was to explain: 'You see, they are not the same as you and me, they think differently, if and when they do think. It's a strange world that they live in and occupy all by themselves.'

I had my documents sent from the Australian military, and before P Company, I had an interview with a specific commanding officer, a British colonel. I thought if I proved I was para-qualified I would get para pay. I did not mind or have any resistance to doing P Company selection. After all I had heard, I was looking forward to it, to see if I would make the grade and get through.

The officer was most understanding as I handed the documents to him. 'Para trained in Oustralia … Yes, well, that's all very well and good.'

I could see him thinking. 'Yes, well anyone can jump out of an aeroplane. Was your plane British or Oustralian?'

'Neither sir, Caribous and C-130s.'

'Yes, exactly, there you have it, not British aeroplanes.'

'No sir, different markings but the same kind.'

'Yes exactly, not British. Anyone can jump out of a plane. It's P Company you see, that's what it's all about … Oustralia you say … we all have great admiration for the Oustralians, but the colonials trained you.'

This was 1969, and we were still a colony! He went back to shuffling papers as if I did not exist and in his world I didn't. That was it: home team 1 – colonials 0.

They are strange in a laboratory sort of way, disconcerting in others. Fascinating indeed, they are a wonder to behold. With regards to the Trogs, I did meet some interesting if not strange people too, some real mad hatters, most if not all incredibly courageous and brave when it came to the job. When I saw some of them walking up the hill in Aldershot towards me on my side of the road, I would cross over, discretion being the better part of valour, not knowing if they were drunk or just having a bad day. I was different. I knew how to do things again. I got on with the training staff. My first encounter was with a very large Scot when in Recruit Company. I can't remember what the problem was; maybe he never liked me. He hit me with a well-placed punch, but, strangely enough, for a big man he never hurt me at all. Everyone held their breath thinking this was it, murder in the ranks. I just stood there, for two reasons: firstly, it was recruit training and I thought maybe they would throw me out, as they had done to many others. I felt at that time that the Brit Paras was my ticket home to Australia. Milling was one thing but fighting and damage to barrack rooms? Not so. I could see my means of getting back home flying out the window. Secondly, it amazed me that such a big man had such a girly punch. I just looked at him and he looked at me then I shrugged and walked away. He never made it through P Company. Believe me, he was big.

I remember most, but not all the members of the platoon, some more than others. Some I liked, some I was indifferent to. I was not there for any other reason than I found soldiering easy, I got paid and fed and could have a hot shower. I would move out once I got to the Far East again. The regiment was my ticket home. I do remember some with fondness, but some of them … well, you can't like everyone, can you?

There also were some unbelievably humorous times. Not only did we have young men from all over England and Wales, but we had lads from Ireland as well as the Jocks from Scotland. In the early days of basic training, one of the Irish lads lost the key to his locker. Inside the steel locker everything was neatly folded, boxed and set out in preordained order. Bedding was stripped down, neatly wrapped and boxed in a tight square at the foot of the bed every morning. Rooms, showers and ablution blocks had to be clean and spotless before we had to stand by our beds shaved, showered and dressed ready for early morning inspections. Barrack-room inspections are everything the movies make them out to be; this they get right. They are terrifying to the uninitiated. A bedside parade can spoil your day, your week and even your life if it goes wrong. Paddy the Irish lad could not get into his locker to square it away, nor could he get his clothes to dress, nor could he shave. Everything was locked securely in the locker. He should have broken the lock, sorted everything out, then later got a new lock, thinking like a civilian which he still was even if he had signed on the dotted line. Should he break the door? He went into a panic thinking about buying a new lock and a new door, then into a mental coma as he pondered. No! He would stand by his bed in his PJs and explain to the officer or sergeant his predicament. 'Any reasonable person would understand,' he said. It was not going to be a good day for any of us. You could hear the footsteps of the entourage drawing near, inspecting sergeant and flanking corporals approaching. Every few paces they would stop, looking at a bed block or a locker in silence. With some small comment when throwing an item on the floor or throwing the whole lot out the window, such as your bedding, with comments such as, 'If you can grab it before it hits the floor it's yours' before moving on to destroy another recruit's life. If I had been Paddy I would have run, simulated a heart attack or an epileptic fit, but no, I could see out the corner of my eye he was standing to attention, head held high and dressed in his PJs. I think at that time his only saving virtue was that the PJs did not have Winnie the Pooh printed on them; they were military issue, so technically he was in uniform, albeit the wrong one for the occasion.

The army has lots of barracks and parade grounds and what one would call MOD property. Civilians could be forgiven for thinking that this equipment and barracks belongs to the government or the Minister of Defence when in the fact it does not. Every square inch of military property belongs to one or other sergeant-major. Parade grounds, company lines, the lot, the only place that does not belong to him is the troops' mess or dining area; he is not allowed in unless invited. Needless to say, if he wants to enter someone had best invite him in. Every regimental area belongs to the Regimental Sergeant-Major. Ask one, or walk across the parade ground and a voice like thunder will tell you to 'Get off *my* parade ground!' If seen, it's 'What are you doing in *my* regiment with a haircut like that?' Alternatively, 'Don't walk across *my* grass' and 'Don't litter *my* barracks' after dropping a Lilliputian postage-stamp-sized speck of something. 'Don't saunter around *my* company; pull your shoulders back, lad!'

We all had visions of the results of the inevitable question. 'What are you doing dressed like that on *my* inspection?' An enquiry delivered with a damaging, aggressive and robust line of questioning, followed by a bed going out through the window, if not a bed then definitely the errant locker and maybe even the troop following close behind it, to be marched off limping to the guardhouse and inevitable jail. Sergeants and sergeant-majors are not easily defeated, nor do they ever cry, or I had not seen it up until then.

The silence was deafening, the kind of silence one hears when walking through the bush or jungle waiting for that first angry shot. When will it come and from where and at whom? No ranting or raised voices, just gentle, mild words.

'What's your name, laddie?' It was a very soft, benevolent voice to start with, the kind one uses on puppies and imbeciles. 'Today you have achieved what the Germans could not achieve at Arnhem. In all my years, not Suez, Cyprus, the Indonesians, or any other smelly Wog, be it in desert or jungle, could have achieved what you have this morning. You, laddie, have left me speechless. Are you deliberately trying to destroy the regiment single-handed?' Then at the top of his voice: 'DON'T YOU LIKE ME, LADDIE? DON'T YOU LIKE ME? I DON'T KNOW WHAT TO DO WITH YOU … YOU'RE A SIGHT. ONE I HAVE NEVER BEHELD BEFORE IN ALL MY YEARS AS A SOLDIER. ARE YOU DELIBERATELY TRYING TO MAKE …' At this point the sergeant started to refer to body parts by way of explanation, his knowledge of the English adjective as poetic as it was repetitious, all delivered in colourful, colloquial descriptions, of various parts of the human anatomy, male and female. Then he stopped, breathless, with little veins pulsating at the side of his neck and turned to walk away. As the entourage left, I was sure I heard a distinct sob, or maybe the start of hysterical laughter, along with what I thought were the words, 'What is my bloody world coming to?' Paddy was gone when we came back from our run. The little man just ceased to exist in the world of the military: Paddy had never really been there.

The strange thing about the British parachute soldier is he is unlike the airborne troops you see in American movies who are all portrayed as hulks having played for the college football team, all sporting haircuts that make their heads look flat and with a steely blue-eyed stare. The Brits are usually tiny little men, many with crooked, nicotine-stained teeth (what the Americans call English teeth). Once they are rigid with a parachute pack on their back and the round steel dome of a helmet on their head, they look like little-Humpty-backed dwarfs and all of them, to a man, have an attitude problem. History has proven that once they go into a fighting frenzy, the only way to stop them is by killing them. Men of the Parachute Regiment are stubborn, wilful and tenacious; I would say out and out bloody-minded bolshie and just very, very difficult, like no other living organism known to man. For no reason, they see themselves as unique or different, and they are because they want to be. English politicians have called them Britain's baby-faced killers and the late Margaret Thatcher was to say if you're going to win a battle send in the Marines and if you're going to win a war send in the Parachute Regiment. They genuinely believe that the maroon beret is bulletproof.

Our platoon sergeant in training was Sergeant Bunny Harvey. Now with a name like Bunny, you would think he would be gentle and kind. Sergeant Bunny looked nothing like a rabbit at all. (The star of the 1950 movie *Harvey* – starring James Stewart – was a white rabbit called Harvey, hence the sergeant's nickname.) Bunny had taken part in the brief campaign known as the Suez Crisis in Egypt in 1956. His chalk lobbed in with the regiment. They exited the door without their reserve 'chutes as they were carrying so much equipment and there was no room to clip on the reserve. They still went out on the green. Bunny got hurt parachuting into Suez. Although a short war, it had its share of firefights. No movie cameras so most, if not all, went unnoticed. Brits were never worried about collateral damage; a plummy voice would say, 'I don't recall, nor do I have any such report of any such action' all with a surprised gentlemanly air 'Surely not! We are British, after all.' Bunny had been there, which was why he was a sergeant instructor.

He was a small man with a little pencil moustachio and walked with a parachute soldier's swagger. This swagger is hard to define; it is pride, self-awareness, cockiness, 'been there done that' and 'I am a Para and what are you going to do about it?' I liked Bunny: he was a good man to learn from and to soldier with.

Then we had Dennehy. He had fought in Borneo, another small war that the Brits have conveniently forgotten. His company, B Company 2 Para, was dug in on the side of a jungle hill when they came under fire, first from heavy mortars before the Indonesians put in their attack and tried to overrun the position. B Company beat them back, and, as the Indonesians retreated down the hill, the platoon came out of their foxholes and conducted a bayonet charge down the mountain after the enemy. In jungle warfare, this is a most unusual operational tactic – it is not healthy to leave a secure position when outnumbered to chase after the enemy when you have just beaten them off. The Indonesian-Javanese battalion suffered fifty deaths and an unknown amount of wounded at the battle of Plaman Mapu; B Company's casualties were two killed and seven injured. Not a bad day's work considering B Company was not even at full strength.

My platoon completed basic training from the depot of the Parachute Regiment and Airborne Forces on 5 December 1969 with only nineteen members left out of a mass of gathered hopefuls when we first mustered on the parade square. How many people dropped out or said it wasn't for them, I don't recall as I didn't count when we first mustered. (Our machine-gunner at a later stage was an ex-Royal Marine, who had been injured by a grenade necklace in Aden. He had convalesced and re-enlisted and went through the full basic training and P Company.)

Newly qualified recruits sent up to one of the regiment's battalions endured verbal assault, intimidation and acts of physical violence. Old soldiers made it clear they were not yet 'real' Paras. Even when you got to a battalion, if you had too much to say, you would end up damaged from falling out of windows or down flights of stairs, a fat lip or black eye being the least of your problems. So, I did what came naturally: I shut my mouth. A new soldier is treated like a day-one, week-one recruit all over again. It is a wonder that they ever keep enough troops to fight in a war.

One does not become a British parachute soldier by going up to a regular battalion. It's something that happens. One day you're a nothing, then you're a Para. It's that day when you stop thinking like a civilian and start to feel and think like a professional parachute soldier. The snooty officer with the plummy voice that sounded as if he had a peg on his nose was right: any fool can exit an aeroplane but few get past P Company. One did have to be determined and incredibly fit if you wanted to get into the Parachute Regiment. The British Army maintains it takes at least eighteen months to make a full-term professional soldier, if before then he has not been shot dead in some distant war or broken any major bones that keep the human body upright. Only after these eighteen months can they get any use out of him.

As a member of 2 Para, I did three tours in Northern Ireland, two as a troop on the ground and one with a small covert group called the MRF (Military Reaction Force). Contrary to popular belief and legend, the MRF was not some highly trained clandestine unit; it was merely a group of soldiers drawn and detached from their parent units to work undercover as civilians. I was de-soldier-fied, for want of a better word, for two or three months before travelling with a partner to Belfast. All this would take place on my last tour.

I went to 2 Para on my return from leave, after passing out from basic training. I was at battalion in early January 1970 and operationally mobilized to move out sometime in February. Silly me, I thought we were going someplace nice before the words Northern Ireland started being muttered amongst the troops. Northern Ireland, Northern Ireland? Isn't that part of the United Kingdom, part of England with people just like us? I found this Ireland thing a bit ludicrous; I knew nothing about what they called The Troubles. I had gone to school with Irish kids, I mean the Catholic Church was awash with them; my grandfather was an Irishman though an unpleasant one. The only time I had heard of The Troubles was from Flip in Australia. His name was Flanagan, but not really. His father had arrived in Australia from Ireland with another handle, sometime in the 1920s and changed his name, having done some things, something to do with the Black and Tans. Once one was in Australia one became a fair dinkum, or true blue, Australian.

I packed for Northern Ireland, any idea of going to a warmer climate squashed. In Ireland we had to sleep in burned-out buildings and even doorways. There was not enough billeting for the Trogs or for anyone else for that matter. The Brits were caught on the back foot as they always are – remember Dunkirk and Singapore. Deployed along with D Company 2 Para, we all ended up sleeping in an old mill, just off the Shankhill Road in Belfast. After a time, we managed to make it habitable and, by the end of the first tour, it was like home. Irish Republican Army (IRA) snipers took shots at our patrols and we took casualties almost straight away. We also employed cordon and search operations, looking for arms. We would find some excellent pieces now and then, real collector's items.

By and large, it was just endless patrol after patrol, day and night, the best being the night patrols. Then the powers that be built a wall between the Protestant and Catholic areas, out of lengths of corrugated sheets about three metres high, so the shooters had to get up high to fire at us. The fence was to keep the two sides apart, the nationalists (Catholics) on one side and the loyalists (Protestants) on the other. I had never come across such animosity. Sectarian and civil wars bring out the worst in people. I could feel the blood-curdling hate from the IRA sympathizers, adults and children alike. It was almost tangible in its completeness.

Once when patrolling the Peace Line – an inappropriate name for the tin wall – I had rounds smacking into a building I passed. One was about ten inches just above my head. We opened up on possible places that the shooter might have been firing from before a mobile patrol went round the back to try and get him, but most times it was shoot and scoot. Another occasion was much the same thing, as two of us went into a burned-out building to get up to a second floor to return fire, I fell through the burned-out floor.

Once on a vehicle patrol, we were directed to a possible ambush site to clear it and cordon off the area. When we got to the top of the road, the sergeant sat for a time then came up with an idea. We could drive slowly towards the area and possibly the bomb would go off before we got to the kill zone and it would miss us altogether. Or we could drive very fast and get past the kill zone before the bomb was detonated. It was a no-brainer – 'Let's stay here until another patrol comes from the other side.' The bomb went off, so we went down to clear and keep people away in case of a secondary device. It was a new kind of war blowing up coffee shops and boys and girls doing terrorist work. For many young soldiers, it was traumatic seeing bomb victims or parts thereof. We have, over time, become desensitized to bombings and body parts thanks to the media. Before Northern Ireland, we had terrorists all across the world but not on the high streets of the UK, and that's what Northern Ireland is, then and now a part of the United Kingdom.

Initially, even finding and retrieving the victims' remains had not been planned for; it was a very ad-hoc arrangement with no proper body bags or procedures. Cordoning off and cleaning up for the very young soldier was highly emotional, and I think damaging for many of them.

Various things happen to a soldier in combat. He can, after time, resign himself to the fact that he is there to do a job, so let's get on and do it. He can adopt the view of what is for you won't go past you. Contact with the enemy can be almost therapeutic, a release valve. It is not the possibility of death that grinds him down; it is the waiting for that one angry shot. Ireland was like nothing else; the soldier only had so many routes he could travel and limited cover to go to if under fire. It was being at the end of a road or turning in to a street that was a hundred yards long, like walking up a shooting range and not knowing if the shooter already had you in his sights. It was the children filled with hate and knowing that although they wanted you dead, should you come under fire, your first thought was the safety of those very children. It was walking past a shop window that could at any second explode and shatter, sending a thousand glass-shard projectiles through the air to cut you in two or lacerate your face and leave you blind forever. It was seeing beautiful young women and strong young men with arms or half a leg blown away. It was the smell of fear from civilians who did not know about killing and war, the brick dust in the air like an old London fog and the crunch of broken glass under your boots. As you went in to find more broken bodies and the silent plea, please, don't let me see any more as I can't stop the bleeding and they will die before the ambulance can get to them, and always the ever-present aroma of cordite and plastic explosives.

Once on a night patrol, three IRA men opened fire on my patrol from the top of a row of houses, hiding behind a chimney stack. Everyone in the patrol had been in Ireland for a time, so we were used to this kind of nonsense, old hands now, not wondering what to do next. We deployed and returned fire fast, too fast for them to move off the roof, so we had them pinned. In military terminology we had won the firefight. All they had to do was yell and tell us they were coming down, so don't shoot. We would have arrested them, sure, and they would have gone to jail for a long time, but they would have been alive. But no. I think it was like a game of Cowboys and Indians to them. They had no idea of the firepower of a six-man patrol, each with an SLR that fires a full metal jacket 7.62 NATO round. So, what do the empty heads do? They keep shooting at us from around the chimney, thinking the brickwork will keep them safe. They could have stopped at any time. We just returned fire and chopped the stack down. Every time a volley hit the brickwork, you heard bits of brick rolling down off the roof. Just one word would have saved them. By this time, another patrol with a young lieutenant arrived. He wanted to talk to them but they would not listen so both patrols opened up. We heard one body bounce down the roof. There was nothing left for them to hide behind. All three went down, one after another. The young lieutenant and a medical officer (a doctor from Medical Corps) went around the other side where they had fallen. All I got over the radio was that it was total carnage. I could hear from the lieutenant's voice that he was disturbed by what he found. One could say they fought to the end when in fact they were just stupid – one word, only one word, and we would have stopped.

My second tour was much the same as the first but this time we were stationed in an old shop right on a corner at a T-junction. The IRA used to put in some very good ambushes, what I would call well-thought-out good concept, well planned but poorly executed. I put this down to almost nonexistent training. Where could they go? All insurgents need a host country where they can train or spend their R&Rs. Ireland is an island and what with the Royal Navy and the Marines, it was difficult for them to move in and out and every bit as difficult for them to ship in equipment and ordnance. Southern Ireland, the Republic, was sympathetic but was not going to get too involved by letting them have training camps, and the Garda kept a close watch on things when it came to the IRA.

One wet Friday night found me taking cover in a shop doorway. I was watching a young couple walking towards me. They were very chatty, arm in arm. The girl was all dressed up for a night out with her young lad, and snuggling up to him to keep warm. Then shots were being fired with rounds bouncing off the brickwork. I now had behind me in my shop doorway this young boy with his girlfriend crouching down, using me as cover. They had been on their way to the pictures. She was crying and all she kept on saying was, 'Dear God, dear God soldier, don't let them kill us.' She was so close trying to take cover, I could smell the fragrance of her washed hair, her make-up, I felt her shaking. I had been on patrol for some time so was cold and I could feel her body heat. It was surreal – someone was about to die and it could be them. Had she thought of that when she had brushed her hair and put on her lipstick? Then the shooting stopped. No crack and thump, no muzzle flash. I moved the patrol and gave them watch and shoot but no one had a target, so we did not return fire. Bullets travel a long way. The patrol continued into the darkness and the two civilians to their night out.

On that second tour, the battalion split down to sections, D Company taking up residence in a location which became our new home. It was in what they call a corner shop, or mom and pop store. We had a private dwelling on one side and storage facilities on the other which was owned and used by another shop in the area. For security reasons the keys for the store were held at our operations centre. Every time an item came into the store, or was delivered, we checked it for anything that could be a danger to our position before it was allowed in. It was in this location that I first would have come under fire from a Thompson sub-machine gun, had it worked. Again, good IRA ideas and planning but woeful application. We had two entrances to our location, one at the front where we had speed ramps and wire, the other that opened into the side street. We alternated using either one of the doors so as not to present a pattern or be stereotyped.

One day the IRA had a plan to place a bomb across from our main entry point, with a gunman kneeling at the corner ready to open fire as soon as troops came out from door number two. Instead of placing the bomb, the bomber threw it over the wall. The detonation device dislodged because of the impact. The gunman with the Thompson opened fire as soon as he saw what was happening. The weapon fired once and then jammed. When we cleared the area, we found one struck round that had not fired and two that had ejected, also not having fired. We think the bomber panicked and threw the bomb. The

Thompson was to open up on the troops as they came out the second door when the bomb went off, but saw that our sentry was about to open up on the bomb thrower, so opened fire, or tried to. Nothing happened after one or two tries so he bugged out. Well thought out, well planned, but poorly executed, and aren't we glad about that.

A tragic conclusion to this story took place some months later. We moved out and rotated back to the UK. Another company from another regiment, not Para, took over. A third party came and asked for the key to the storeroom; the new section put in the same security of checking everything that came in as we had. After a short time, they became familiar with the third party and just handed him the key. One day someone infiltrated a whole lot of wooden egg crates packed with explosives, and the storeroom and the house were razed to the ground. Most of the section was out on patrols, and only a small complement was in the house at the time, so it could have been worse.

In August 1971, I took part in Operation Demetrius, implementing detention and internment without trial. Demetrius ticked the IRA off in a big way, and for the following three days it was out-and-out street fighting. We had disrupted their chain of command, and without control from the more experienced fighters, the younger members of the IRA thought they could take us on. They engaged us in open warfare. Within the first forty-eight hours the death toll had reached seventeen. We were on the streets for seventy-two hours, either on foot or in the Saracen armoured vehicles. It was too lethal on the streets for lightly armoured Land Rovers. Some say internment helped, others think it was counterproductive. It never sat comfortably with me just entering a man's home and taking him away, especially in front of a wife and kids. As a soldier, I did what I had to do.

I think it was internment that led to Operation Motorman in 1972. By early 1972, the IRA had established twenty-nine barricaded no-go areas, of which sixteen were utterly impassable. These locations were controlled respectively by the Provisional IRA and the Official IRA. The IRA detonated twenty-two bombs within seventy-five minutes; eleven people were killed, among them British troops, with 130 injured. Operation Motorman took place ten days later. The barricades were breached by tanks with their guns covered, along with armoured bulldozers. The surge of troops was overwhelming; they faced little resistance. The IRA ran an insurgency war of armed propaganda; it was ill-equipped for open warfare against such a large force. No attempt was made by them to hold ground, and by the end of the day, all the no-go areas in Derry and Belfast had been cleared of barricades. The army would have to remain for some time and still have to move with caution when operating in staunchly Republican districts. Official documents reveal that Operation Motorman was the most significant British military operation since the Suez Crisis of 1956 and the biggest in Ireland since the Irish War of Independence of 1919–1921.

When I first joined the British Army, we used to have to march up to a table, salute the officer and count our pay, in cash. We got paid weekly (as well as weakly). Then the banks got an idea and put it to the MOD that we should be paid directly from a bank account. So, the military reviewed the whole method of payments. A Trog used to get all his uniforms free and exchanged if damaged, food and accommodation provided at no cost, plus travel warrants whenever he went on leave. Troops use to get lots of stuff free, but not much money. Then they readjusted the pay scale, taking into consideration that we would now only have two clothing issues, all others paid for, which would stop theft and Trogs selling off bits of equipment (which they thought theirs by default; they had been given it by the young green officer and had had it for so long that it surely must be theirs). The Trogs would also have to pay for accommodation, no more warrants etc. Some bean counter sat and worked out how much such things were worth and monetized everything. It got so bad that local pubs and watering holes would no longer accept cheques from anyone in case the cheques had been written out by a Trog. Shops demanded cash, and even the banks made one wait in line to cash a cheque, while they perused statements to see if the account did indeed have sufficient funds. It affected the more mature men who had families as well as those who did run proper banking accounts. It got so painful that the Army Pay Corps had to come and give lessons in money management. A regiment of Paras, each with a cheque book, can't destroy the banking system in England, but they went a long way in disrupting the upward climb of some bank managers. It was to the benefit of the banks as they got lots of money from the government, but not so helpful for the pubs and shops that almost went broke. It was the closest thing to purgatory local bank managers were to experience. The bean counters who concocted this system had omitted one intangible: soldiers go off to war. If he is sleeping on the floor or in a doorway or trench, you can't charge for his billet. You still have to feed him at your cost, and you can't make him buy his uniform if it has been burned by a petrol bomb or torn in performing whatever duty in an operational role, be it jungle, street or desert. All our money was suddenly ours.

Personally, the three tours were right for me. We had debarkation leave before shipping out. Most everyone with a home to go to went home. I went across to Europe on vacation. It was very much the same when we came back and stood down. The locals went home on leave and painted the kitchen or built a new garden shed; I, on the other hand, rented a villa in southern Spain for three weeks accompanied by a little WRAC who came on leave with me. The army was turning out to be not too bad. Not only in the travel when on vacation, but my gaining first-hand experience and knowledge acquired when working in a hostile urban environment. Ireland was an entirely different environment to the jungle, a role I had initially trained for with the Australians. By my second deployment, I had been promoted, not to dizzy heights but in the right direction: up. At some time, I must have done something right as I was offered a freefall parachute course with the Red Devils. A freefall course is a very prestigious course. I learned to freefall out of an old de Havilland Rapide biplane built in the 1930s. It could take about eight freefallers; my freefall certificate has 'Army Parachute Centre Netheravon Wiltshire' printed on it. The course was run and completed in Northern Ireland, so I could say when on active service with the Parachute Regiment I was to freefall into an operational area, although I think that would be stretching it. On all my leaves I travelled around Europe. I had worked Laos out of my psyche, or so I thought. It was a wonderful time of my life. I toured with the knowledge I had a home to come back to, and just as I was getting bored with it all, another deployment to Ireland came up. Also, I had most weekends off and The Shot (Aldershot) is only a short train ride into London.

I used to stay in the centre of London at the Union Jack Club. It was a hotel for British troops, well run and spanking clean and right bang in the middle of theatreland. We could also get tickets for all the live stage shows in London for almost nothing. I think that would have pleased Kipling, and they were some of the best seats in the house as well, which would have pleased Private Thomas Atkins. Not many Trogs went in to London as most went home so I always got a nice room and a ticket for something at a reasonable price. I never did get around to thanking the IRA, as without their help, none of this would have been possible.

My last tour of Ireland more or less started back at Aldershot at that time home to the Parachute Regiment. I was called to the boss's office and asked if I would be interested in doing something different on my next duty in Ireland. I was to be detached from the regiment and attached to something or other, at that time I knew not what. I volunteered as the idea of undercover work sounded interesting. From that day on clearance was given to wear civilian clothes. No more haircuts, in fact not to act like I was a Tom (troop) at all. Things were going well for me: no duty as such, no parades and my de-soldiering was advancing to the point where I really looked like a civilian, or so I thought. Then one day, roaming through the lines, I heard a voice behind me; it was not God speaking but the closest thing to God that the Parachute Regiment has.

'Come here laddie.'

I kept on walking, hands in pockets.

'You laddie, you with your wee hands in your pockets, come to me, that's an order.'

You have to understand the mental state of a regimental sergeant-major. It is *his* regiment. He allows the colonel to play with the troops and move battalions around. However, when in barracks, soldiers and equipment belong to him, even the scruffy wee lad with his paws in his pockets. I walked over to him.

'And what was that?'

'What was what, sir'?

'That.' He pointed where I had just walked from. 'You get back over there and when I call you, you will march, laddie; you will march and move smartly and briskly and come to attention in front of me, right where you're standing now. Not an inch to the right or left, on that very spot you're on right now.' Did he know whether I was, in fact, a soldier or just a lost civilian? Had my de-soldiering not worked?

Soldier (me) turned and walked, feeling self-conscious and more than a little awkward, and turned again, facing and looking at a very, very cross RSM. He did not say much other than 'March!' Like some errant child I did just as ordered. I marched – tick-tock, tick-tock – and came to a screeching halt, slamming my foot into the ground as I came to attention. An act that was somewhat painful as I was in civilian clothes and wearing a nice pair of brown loafers, not military-issue boots.

'Look down at your wee feet, laddie.'

The laddie (me) looked down and saw nothing other than his painful feet.

'I told you, on the same spot, did I not?'

'Sir.'

'Why are you mumbling soldier? What's your name?'

That's it. He wanted to know who I was; only death could save me now. I gave number, rank and name. 'Right, corporal, I want you to go back the way you came, smart like a soldier. Then I want you back here on the very spot I asked you to come to attention on, not an inch to the right or left, not back or forward, but here!' He tapped the ground with his pace stick, a sizeable wooden compass that is set out or opened to a regulation-sized marching step. By that time, we had a small audience standing some way off, not wanting to get too close unless they became collateral damage. I turned and went through the whole idiotic procedure again, and again, several times.

'Now I want you to disappear from my sight, and at 1800 hours you will be outside the guardroom dressed in full walking-out dress, with a haircut. You will then parade at 2200 hours and then again at 0200 hours and again at 0600 hours, and then I shall decide what we shall do with you.'

I thought he had dismissed me, so I started to move.

'Where do you think you're going, soldier?'

'Back, to the lines, sir.'

'You don't think for one second I am going to allow you anywhere near real soldiers, do you?'

'No, sir.'

'You're not going to walk around my camp looking like that. Find some other way or stay where you are until it's dark.'

I waited a respectful time then went to see my boss; he put in a call to the RSM, to inform him without giving a great deal of detail of why I was walking around looking like a total disgrace to the regiment and still being allowed to breathe. The RSM's only request was that they kept me out of his sight and away from other troops so I would not infect them.

Some weeks later, I left by boat for Northern Ireland as a civilian. I was met at the docks by a team all equally as scruffy as me. I would work out of a compound inside Palace Barracks, or Hollywood as we sometimes called it. In one corner of this restricted area was a grave with a name chalked on a headstone. I asked who was in there. 'No one yet, we're still looking for him.' I thought that rather bizarre but it was the way things were run, entirely off the wall. I had found a lot of new wackos, the kind not seen since Laos. I had found a new home.

The MRF had various names, but I always knew it as the Military Reaction Force. I worked in what the Brits called mufti, or plain clothes, to blend in. I learned very quickly that in this kind of job, it was no good pretending you are something or acting when working covert; your life depends on you *being the real thing*. You have to become what they are. Pretend or acting, people will see through you. When you're in the middle of a crowd of IRA supporters, you *are* a supporter. I was an Australian, a good wee Catholic lad at that who had a grandfather called O'Bryant. An authentic colonial boy and I lived it. When you walk down the road behind the coffin with a thousand people, at a gunman's funeral, you are a mourner. You live what you are meant to be; anything less leads to torture and horrible death. Something you don't deserve because you are on their side and you are one of them. Annihilation can come from either party at any time. We would, from time to time, employ some strange and peculiar methodology. That would include but was not limited to such actions as hiding machine guns inside shopping bags – being a tourist from overseas or sleeping in bombed-out buildings on ops.

Two of us were in fact in a bombed-out building. We had had a tip that they, the IRA, would be coming back as it was an antique shop and the safe was still intact, sitting in the downstairs office. We sat in the dark then heard a vehicle pull up and people entering the site. Let them come right in then we'll take them down. A torch probed the darkness; it danced around and illuminated two firefighters. Why would we shoot two firefighters? We would not. We spoke out of the night and made ourselves known then had a short conversation, something along the lines of what the devil are you doing here? They were part of the fire crew that had attended to the explosion. They had come back to look. At what? The safe, silly. We sat and talked with our new conspirators: did they know anyone who could open it? In the end, they went back to the fire station and came back with a fire engine. They had left all the hoses back at the station. I had no idea just how much space is in or under a fire engine. I looked inside – it was like a cave. It was suggested to leave the safe for later and just clean out what they could. After being blown up, an antique shop has nothing left that is worth having. The shop next door, however, had been damaged but not gutted, and it had all kinds of stuff. We were there to shoot someone so we stayed on station. We would see them later after we worked out where exactly we could put our new TV sets that the fire station donated to us. They had two new TV sets that were not needed as they already had … quite a few. The safe, when opened, was empty but the shop owner put in a substantial claim. I explained to him that I knew the safe was empty before, as we had opened it. It was terribly dishonest of him, and we could always take it back as evidence. The next leave I hired a villa in Spain for three weeks

We gathered intelligence, looked for bad people, instigated incidents which would result in an arrest or shooting. Or we simply did our job. There were times of dark humour, such as the time I walked up to a vehicle. The driver turned to face me and, seeing the pistol in my hand just as I was standing at the window, put foot and sped away, forgetting about anyone else. I opened fire at the vehicle: lousy move as a hundred metres down the road was an army checkpoint. The next thing I heard was the crack of 7.62 rounds as they passed by me, slamming against the wall where I was standing with gun in hand. I was being shot at by my fellow troops. Fortunately, it was nighttime and in those days, or nights, there was very little hi-tech night-vision equipment. The team member I was with went ballistic at me. Some of the incoming rounds had come very close to him. The next morning, I was called into the boss's office. I told him what had happened. He was a captain,

I think, in the Brit SAS. He had his little chat with me and ended it with 'Jolly good, well done.' He confirmed what I already thought our job was about. To this day, I still don't know who he was, only from where he came.

I carried a Browning Hi-power 9mm pistol and a Sterling machine pistol of the same calibre; we were also given Ingrams, an American-made weapon, again a hand-held machine pistol with a silencer (suppressor). It was only ten and a half inches long, and without the suppressor screwed on, difficult to fire. They later took them back off us as they said it was a gangster's weapon. English can be strange people. Does it matter what you kill the enemy with as long as he is dead?

I had one very embarrassing and almost lethal experience with the Sterling. I carried it in a shopping bag, just an everyday ordinary paper bag with agreeable patterns printed on it. I was walking around Belfast; it was raining as usual, so I went into a shop to stay out of the weather. As I entered, I heard a metallic clunk. Looking down, I could see the barrel of the Sterling sticking through a hole in the bottom of the wet paper shopping bag. All that was stopping it from falling right the way through and on to the floor was the magazine. I apologized to the ladies in the shop, turned and walked back out into the rain, with the bag now tucked under my arm.

The people I worked against were ruthless. They bordered on the savage and even psychotic, nothing subtle about them at all. Had they caught any of us, as they did once or twice, we would have ended up dumped near an army post dead, and that would have been the best part of it. We operated in two-man teams; four young men in a car had as much chance of being shot by the Brits as by the IRA, too conspicuous. Our operations never called for reports and were never recorded. I don't think it is of any benefit to extrapolate or expand too much on my operational role with the MRF, but some of them were more innocuous than others. Once we had a mobile laundry van that collected items for cleaning.

We did forensics on them before anything was cleaned. The vehicle, in the end, was shot up by IRA gunmen, and we hold the dubious record of being the only military unit to have had a WRAC troop killed when working undercover. I have never been able to confirm the operation or the death of the female operative – she may have come from the Ulster Defence Regiment, or any one of a dozen covert units that at some time or other were operational. Then again, I would not be able to confirm many of the ops I did, as no one used their real names and it was not done to even ask what unit he or she had served with before coming to the MRF.

One incident I don't place at anyone's feet and don't even give a location or date to, but know without any doubt took place, was when an unknown gunman was shot off a roof, during a riot. He was dressed in black and had a Colt AR-7 collapsible rifle, a survival rifle favoured by US pilots should they have to punch out. This little .22 is not a weapon of war but is deadly accurate and if suppressed can drop someone next to you, without you even knowing they are down, or from what direction the shots had come. It was just a matter of waiting for him. We figured his job was to shoot at troops so they would return fire and cause a political incident. Intelligence informed me through an unknown someone – the unknown could have been from Disneyland for all I knew – that the dead body when alive had come from one of the Eastern bloc countries over ten years ago and had worked for the postal service. So, if your mail was late, you now know why. If anyone is missing a foreign-speaking or Soviet postman, who you gonna call?

We also ran a massage parlour, not me personally of course but it was there; that also got compromised in the end. The problem with working covert in Northern Ireland was you had families that had lived in the same house and street for years, maybe two or even three or four generations. Many married the girl in the next road down or around the corner. They were interrelated or had known one another from when they were children. Strangers were noticed.

We had a client who was neither pro-IRA nor pro-British. He just wanted to be left alone, but he knew lots. The man was just sick and tired of having windows broken at his business by bombings, and his life disrupted all the time. The IRA leaned on him to become an active member, but he was not interested. The army wanted him on their side to help them, but he would not play. He was a fence-sitter, but how to get him off the fence? Simple: blow off his front door early one morning and make him think it was the IRA. Sometimes it was a fun job. We were, in the end, becoming as unsavoury as the IRA. I was once again involved with an organization that had evolved from intelligence-gathering to waging war without interference, but it was all smoke and mirrors. It had to be. After all, surely the British would not use such diabolical methods as has been suggested, being gentlemen and all? The one thing I did learn when working undercover with the Brits is they are ruthless when it comes to the Defence of the Realm. The Russians are brutish, the Americans a bit like Al Capone and the Brits are cold, able, ready and willing. Should difficult people drop around the world, just check you don't see a big black car with a bumper sticker saying I ♥ HEREFORD on the back as it speeds away. The British will kill you with such finesse and aplomb that if you could call from the grave, you would thank them.

I was with the MRF until I was demobbed later in 1972 and returned to the UK. Sometime after I moved on, the MRF was disbanded, or it changed its name. The conflict would carry on for a long time after I left. At the time of the official ceasefire over 3,600 people would be dead – people who looked and dressed just like me.

Chapter 5

Rhodesia: Into the Cauldron

Peace is that brief glorious moment in history when everybody stands around reloading.

Pungwe River, Mozambique (post-ambush)

I am sitting with my back resting against my Bergen, some low foliage supporting it. I watch two young SAS troops trying to get a body into the large plastic bag. A lot of thought has gone into the removal and identification of dead terrorists in this war. One idea was to sling a net under the chopper and lift the bodies out for fingerprinting and identification by the CID. Helicopter pilots did not like the idea, so we don't do it. Another option was just to dump them on the floor, but we got flak from the technician/door gunner, as he had to clean up the mess. We then went on to body bags, an expensive item when used in large quantities, and they also have to be cleaned. We now use big bin bags made out of more durable black plastic than standard rubbish bags, but cheaper than zippy body bags; the downside is it has only one opening, at the top. To try and slide a dead body, a 'floppy', into the mouth of the bag is difficult and takes practice, which I can see the young troopers don't have … yet. They are trying to keep clean, avoiding the mangled bits.

I walk over to help, speaking in a low voice: 'What are you doing? He is already fucking dead. Open the mouth of the bag and keep it on the ground then roll him in. Stuff the separate bits in after.' I go back and sit. They have the general idea. I leave them to it, but they still try and keep clean … it's not going to happen – it's a dirty job.

After my mother had put such an effort into getting the family into Australia, a land of safety – just in the nick in time as we beat the rush – why was I sitting in Mozambique with a four-man ambush team and support elements deep inside a country that borders Rhodesia? From the early 1960s, Africa north of the Limpopo River was not the right place for a white boy to be. As a professional soldier, when I came out of the British Parachute Regiment in 1972, instead of going back to Australia or South East Asia (I had already been there), I headed for Africa. There are only four reasons to go to Africa: one is to make money, two is to make more money. Three and Four are the same as reasons one and two.

Having left the British Parachute Regiment, I started to post adverts in *The Times* of London: 'Looking for work. Parachute/ Special Forces Soldier interested in a lucrative position, will travel.' In the perverse world we live in I did attract some extraordinary job offers. I think the term 'position' is not the right word to use: it can have connotations, even more so in London where diplomats, politicians and Ruperts from the Guards reside. I also got my fair share of 'Let's send you to some far-flung corner of the uncivilized world where you will have no toilets and lots of diseases, to save the primitive.' I met people who kept on telling me there was plenty of work in southern Africa; they were pretty vociferous about it. I don't think we understood one another. When I say work, it had an entirely different connotation to what they were espousing. It did not mean I was going to be driving nails into bits of wood.

A colonel in the South Africa Army had made the statement that should the South African Defence Force (SADF) need more troops to defend South Africa, he was willing to use mercenary soldiers as had been the case in the Congo. The South African spokesman was, however, misreported. What he had said in reply to a question from a local South African journalist was that the SADF had enough troops and would *not* need to use mercenary soldiers as in the Congo. However, it came out in the British tabloids that South Africa was burning – Help! Something got lost in the translation from Afrikaans into English. This I found out when I got to South Africa. I spent a year in South Africa looking for 'work'. I was informed that people like me were not welcome in the Republic, so I left but I was just not ready to return to Australia at that time. I arrived back in the UK with absolutely no idea as to what I would do next. Most assuredly, I could not get on a plane and go back to South Africa; given time, they would need people like me, then I would go back: the South Africans thought they were impervious to the future problems of Black Africa at that time. But what would I do until then? As a family, we had passed through South Africa when moving to Rhodesia. That was in the early 1960s shortly after the Wind of Change speech given by the Harold Macmillan, speaking as a guest in the South African Parliament in 1960. This wind of change ushered in the start of the Cold War on the African continent. The West was trying to appease the not-so-noble savages, hoping they would be pro-West. The communists were doing likewise, hoping to woo the newly 'liberated' and that they would fall into the Soviet sphere of influence. The Cold War between the proxies of East and West was warming up. From 1960, Africa became a tale of horror, of unbridled barbarity and lust for power that would lead to millions of deaths.

What was South Africa's response to the winds of change blowing across Africa, which facilitated the handover of economically viable countries to vast swathes of illiterate and primitive people? To South Africa which had fought the mighty British Empire to a standstill during the Anglo-Boer War, very little. At most, it was an annoying draught through the halls of Afrikanerdom. Africa was burning, and the blacks were killing wholesale long before the second Indochina War when the US got involved in Vietnam. Africa became a slaughterhouse. The Americans abandoned the South Vietnamese and went home in 1973. The western world left Africa to savagery but the white South Africans, unlike the Americans in Vietnam, had no home to flee to.

A coincidence occurred when I got off the tube in London. I was going to South Africa House but I went the wrong way and ended up in front of what was once called Rhodesia House, closed now since UDI, the Rhodesian unilateral declaration of independence in 1965 when diplomatic relations were terminated. It appeared there was a demonstration in progress. On the opposite side of the road was a group of people who seemed very vocal and angry. To my mind not very nice people, with long hair, sandals and no knickers, a 'rent a crowd'. On my side of the road, a slightly smaller group that seemed a little more rational. I stood for a time and seeing that the group on my side of the road were not so agitated, I engaged one person in conversation. He appeared to be safe and pretty innocuous. He wore horn-rimmed glasses, was not very big and had more of a thoughtful look than that of a thug. He had shoes on. He told me that they were supporting a hard-pressed country called Rhodesia. I said I knew the country. He asked me what it was like. I gave him an abridged version and ended by asking what the problem was with the people on the other side of the road. My feet were getting cold just standing there and I was getting ready to move on. But I was curious, so I listened. He asked if I was on vacation. I mentioned I was ex-Brit Para. Mistake.

He grabbed my arm: 'You must go back to Rhodesia; they need people like you!'

It was nice to feel needed, so I went back to Rhodesia. The Rhodesians would pay me once there. How I got there was of little interest to them. Two days later I was no longer unemployed. I caught the ferry across to Europe; I had a job and was on my way to work, admittedly not with a cut lunch sitting on the local 97 bus, but off to work nevertheless.

On my arrival in Rhodesia I would get fully reimbursed for the airline ticket; it was money in the bank. I was taking some of my military kit and equipment with me. There were no direct flights to Rhodesia so I would have to re-route through South Africa, a country that had recently asked me to leave. I had some concerns about that, but moving items of military kit across borders was no problem. Vast numbers of young people were wandering the globe at that time on what was loosely called the hippy trail and I looked like some scruffy reprobate with his home on his back. Going overland was also of more interest, providing insight as to what I might be facing in the future. South Africa was superficially a first world country. North of their borders not so: it was darkest Africa and getting darker.

On my overland trip, I was to spend time travelling through some of the world's most violent and dysfunctional states that were representative of the New African Dawn. The so-called independent African states were sliding into chaos and mayhem. I arrived in Rhodesia via Kazungula, colloquially called Crooks' Corner, as the four countries of Zambia, Rhodesia, Botswana and the Caprivi Strip of South West Africa come together at that point. Poachers in the old days would escape the police or district administrators by hopping from one country to the next, very much like the Golden Triangle in Laos. I don't mean the topography or the drugs but more the coming together of countries forming a geographical triangle. I crossed the Zambezi much the same as I had paddled across the Mekong some years back, only this time it was a rickety African ferry, not a rickety Lao barge. I was back in the country that my mother had tried so desperately to get us all out of. I crossed into Rhodesia in July 1973 and I was to stay until the country was handed over to the communists. I left in November 1980, seven years later.

I became a trooper in the SAS for the most basic of reasons: they gave me the job. They paid me to get there, paid me when I was there, and I genuinely believed then as I still do today that they needed all the help they could get. As with the Americans in Vietnam, the Rhodesians did not lose their war militarily; they lost it politically. They thought they were fighting AK-wielding terrorists, when in fact they were the bulwark against encroaching African savagery and communism. Rhodesia was a country on the very edge of extinction and fighting for its survival. They were in the way of the Globalist Elite; they had to go. The Rhodesians thought all they had to do was keep on fighting, act honourably and eventually the world would understand. Most people were labouring under the delusion that they would win. The political leaders were not so sure, the timing in their minds was they could hold out for ten years.

I completed selection successfully and their parachute course – yes, another one – and I became a badged member of the Special Air Service, allowed to wear the SAS badge, beret and SAS wings. I took part in what were termed cross-border operations into Mozambique and north into Zambia and anywhere else the higher-ups wanted the Special Air Service to go and sometimes even to places where we were not asked to go. Although the SAS in Rhodesia fought mainly a counter-insurgency bush war, we were trained to tackle anything from urban counter-terrorism to covert operations behind enemy lines. Seldom were we used in an infantry role.

The SAS worked in two- or four-man patrols. It sounds as if we were looking for annihilation with such small call signs, but two or four men are easier to hide. We were not infantry; our line function was totally different. We took the fight to the enemy on his home turf, long-range reconnaissance, ambushing and camp attacks. Most all our operations were taking place outside of Rhodesia. My first operation was in a two–man patrol, a soft op, normal mine-laying and reconnaissance. I was teamed up with a captain to do a recce in 'Porkers' (i.e. Portuguese East Africa, or Mozambique). It was the only job I ever did with him as it was his last before leaving for a new life in England. Maybe he knew something I didn't.

Working in small teams meant you got to carry a lot. I experienced a situation where I had no room in my Bergen to fit an extra small radio battery, so I put it in my side pocket. My complement when on external ops was an AK-47 (or FN rifle on specified ops), eight fully charged rifle magazines with two extra bandoliers of fifty rounds, and a pistol with at least four magazines. A four-man team or an ambush patrol would take an extra five or more belts of link for the GPMG as well as British 36 and white phosphorus grenades. I liked the South Africa mini claymore and on my later ambushes I carried six. Also taken were green and red smoke for markers (or extra phosphorus grenades that could be used for marking), a mini-flare, a fighting knife or axe, plus some specialized equipment for hot extraction. That was the business end of it. I then had my navigation equipment – no GPS at that time as it was all done with compass, map and protractor and a bit of string. Then a torch, waterproof notebook (homemade with waterproof tape over the pages or cut-out plastic), writing implements, maps with no markings on them, strobe light and assorted ground-to-air stuff if you were lucky enough to know someone overseas who would buy it for you. Rhodesia fought a war on a shoestring budget. Many troops would go into a gun shop called Feredays in Salisbury (now Harare) and have their webbing made up. I had brought with me the original Bergen I had been issued with when in 2 Commando, an A-frame type. When I had it in Laos everybody wanted one, as it was superior to the American Alice Pack.

Most special forces, due to the amount of equipment they carry, adapt and use what works for them. It was no less so in Rhodesia. Everyone carried their own medical Sosegon (a morphine-derivative painkiller), drips, field dressings, malaria tablets, clean socks and foot medication powder. I was big on socks and foot powder and always had spares in a watertight plastic bag. I can go on forever as long as I have warm, dry feet. All this before we got to personal kit and rations, such as sleeping bag, groundsheet and small gas cooker. Some dickhead told me to paint the blue gas cylinder for my cooker; I just put it in a water bottle carrier. I never used mess tins. I had an old Brit 56 water bottle and tin mug and I did all my cooking out of that. The list of personal equipment had no hard and fast rules; I knew guys who never used a sleeping bag, or would drop some kit just to take extra water or ammunition. Most of your home comforts you left back at your firm base.

My Bergen would weigh thirty kilograms-plus. When I deployed by parachute the jumpmaster/dispatcher would have to help me forward and hold on to me as he moved me to the door: my Bergen was anchored under my reserve 'chute which made me front heavy. With so much weight on the front of my body, had he not held me back, I would have just toppled forward out the opening. I had an American ask how does a two-man team take on a large force and stay alive carrying all that stuff. Most times, we didn't; it was a case of shoot and scoot. We did try to do the job without being compromised, and therein lies the skill of special forces operators: get in, do the job and get out before they even know you have been there. There is nothing to say you can't stash your kit while doing the job – and anyway, thirty kilograms is not so heavy when the adrenalin is pumping.

* * *

A young lieutenant issued a warning order for a patrol into Mozambique; he briefed each member individually. When he had finished briefing me, he took out a little tin box and asked, 'Do you want one of these?' I asked him what for. 'In case something goes wrong.' I realized he was not being pleasant; it was not a sweet he was offering. I told him no thanks. With my kind of luck, I would swallow it at the wrong time, thinking it was a mint, or just lose the bloody thing as it was so small. What would I say when I got back? 'Sorry I lost your poison pill'?

Four of us then deployed by helicopter. The pilot did three or four dummy landings then dropped down with his nose facing north; we were out and clear of the LZ into the thick bush before he had cleared the treetops. Our task was to locate a large terrorist camp. On the second day we got compromised and had to go to ground.

We found a depression in the middle of thick primary foliage. We spent all day listening to them trying to find us, calling and whistling to each another. Toward late afternoon they gave up. We had a democratic meeting and each man was asked what he wanted to do: stay or cut away and make his way back to Rhodesia. Ted and Johnny voted to bug out. Chris asked me what my vote was. I replied that if we left now, it would only mean coming back later. He split the team. It was no problem – that's how we operated.

The next morning the two of us picked up heavy spoor and started to make our way in down a track, for a close-in recce. It couldn't happen to two nicer people but we got compromised again. I was behind Chris who was over six foot, and all I saw was him back-tracking to the left, back into the thick bush, he with legs like a racehorse and me short and stumpy, with my legs pumping like little pistons to try and keep up as a few shots were fired. We ran and walked very fast until nightfall then went to ground. Next day we set a bearing for Rhodesia and pushed for home.

I did a lot of recce patrols, some camp attacks and had lots of 'lemons' (aborted ops – when we got there they had gone). I patrolled with a young officer called Marty. I really like him. Moving slowly in the bush, you get to see a lot of game or the lead scout does. If Marty came across game, he would stop and call me forward and show me what he had seen, tell me what it was and its habits. He should have been a teacher; he was an exceptionally mild man but one who had a determination to kill when it was called for. Not a charismatic person or what one would call a natural leader, he really wanted to be a competent officer. When he went to do the exam for his captaincy, we talked, him telling me he had to pass if his career was to go forward: others were advancing faster than him. I could always imagine him making a total cock-up and then standing in front of you saying, 'I'm sorry; I shall try harder next time' when most people would just say 'Sod it' it and walk away. He made captain; he just wanted to be a good officer. He was later killed in action.

I found myself operating with a small four-man call sign, working externally. The patrol consisted of me, from the Australian Special Forces and late of the British Parachute Regiment; the staff sergeant was from 22 SAS in the UK, and like me had come to Rhodesia for work; a South African named Joe (later killed in action); and a young 20-year-old Rhodesian (also later KIA) who had just returned from a sea voyage with his new fiancée, with whom he was madly in love as he never stopped talking about her. Our four-man team, call sign Papa Four Zero, had been inserted into Porkers some days before. We then got a recall: we were to form up with two other call signs, each of four men and make up a twelve-man ambush team. The ambush commander was the young lieutenant called Marty. We went into our ambush after a long walk in, not wanting to use air or ground support that might have compromised the operation. Our orders were to ambush and bring the whole terrorist group to a final and favourable conclusion, a euphemism for killing anything and everything that ventured into our killing ground, with no returns. We were not interested in prisoners. We were sent to make a point and to leave a couple of identifiable Rhodesian objects behind so that they would know it was the Rhodesians who had done the deed, sending a clear message that no matter how far they withdrew into another country, we would still find and kill them, which we did, successfully I may add. As we moved into the ambush site, my call sign took up position as detailed on the right-hand side of the killing ground, as a cut-off group. I would put in and work the claymore mines. I used to like that; I was good at it. Covering my boots so as not to leave any spoor, I moved forward slowly and, without entering the killing ground directly, I positioned six claymores.* I positioned

---

* A claymore mine is an effective and devastating ambush weapon. Ours came in two sizes, one the American M18 claymore and the other a South African-produced claymore named the mini claymore. The American mine is slightly larger than the South African but the South African mine has more oomph. The material or propellant used and the type of metal or shrapnel sent at high speed into the killing ground

two mines facing up the track, the way we anticipated the enemy would come, two more facing directly away from my call sign to catch any who would try and run away from us into the bush, or turn and run into our position, with the last two placed pointing into the riverbed, my killing ground. Because the track ran down and along a small dry riverbed, I positioned the claymores against the bank. I thought they were a little bit too near me. I told Ted about this, but he was confident that the riverbank would shield us from any backblast. A short distance to my left the same procedure was played out by the killing group overlooking the main killing ground; the left-hand cut-off group on our left flank did the same. Then we waited.

I think it was on the third day that I saw Ted motion to me that we had movement coming in. Our call sign was very close together. Even though the riverbed was dry at that time of year, we had good cover in the thick riverine bush. Our four-man team was close enough to touch one another at arm's length. I saw Ted look down at the handset on the radio and knew the gooks would be arriving at any second. He then started to press down the pressel switch. The pressel switch is a lever on the handset. The handset looks much like a telephone handset, but has a lever on it. When you want to talk on the air, you squeeze down the lever which enables you to speak to another receiver on the same frequency. When the pressel switch is pressed other receivers on the same wavelength hear a tiny click. In an ambush, no one moves or makes any sound. Command elements would hold the handset close to them to avoid any movement or noise. Ted would be able to let the other groups in the ambush

---

are somehow more devastating. I used both types. The South African claymore was smaller and lighter, but its killing ability was far superior to the American mine. The mine itself was not flat but curved, convex on one side and concave on the other, the shape being somewhat like a banana. Printed or embossed into the body of the mine are the words THIS SIDE TO THE ENEMY. Critical instructions; for some reason, the uninitiated always face the claymore the wrong way.

know that the enemy was coming in, and count the numbers. So, prearranged signals might be three very fast, close-together clicks, to alert the team leader that the terrorists were coming in. Then after that, every click would count as one terrorist passing that cut-off point into the killing ground. Although one cannot usually hear the static click when you push down the pressel switch, I listened to every click from Ted, and that was over the thumping of my heart. It sounded as loud as a bass drum; how the gooks could not hear the *thump, thump,* I don't know, it was so loud, and I was so close to them. Then I started to worry. Had I camouflaged the wires and the claymores well enough? The enemy were all looking down at their feet as they walked. I had done ambushes before, and most times we only got one or two, as they splintered once you initiated. This group approaching was a significant number, not the largest, but enough to make it attractive. We would hit larger bodies in the future, but for now, this would do: it was substantial and worth the walk. The group was bunched up like a string of sausages, each linked together as they passed. I could smell them; it was almost as if I could reach out and knock their hats off and hit them over the head with my rifle. I was counting the clicks of the radio: Ted was up to fifteen, sixteen, click, click, and click number twenty-two. I started to wonder if the main killing group had gone to sleep.

Should I pop the claymores? I was watching Ted to give me the go. He was still counting. Then the dull *crump* of explosions as claymores detonated: one of the groups down the track had opened the ambush. I hit the button on my claymores. One second, I had people in front of me, then they just disappeared in a cloud of dust. Now there were a lot of terrorists or what was left of them down in front of me. Gee, I was good at my job. And the hyenas would not go hungry that night. I knew the claymores had been too close. I had dust in my eyes, up my nose, and twigs, and bits of branches were falling down the back of my shirt. For that brief second, I could see nothing; everyone and everything had disappeared. Then we all opened fire into the killing zone. We took some return fire, but I don't think there was anyone down there with much enthusiasm to shoot back. They were falling like dominoes.

Then I heard Ted yelling, 'Move to the high ground. They're flanking us and are going to try and roll us up.' We got to the high ground. We looked down; there were dozens of them. I could hear Ted talking, but my ears were ringing off the hook. High volume, close rifle fire, along with explosions, does that to you. I told Ted I knew the claymores had been too close. Then things settled down, and we waited to see what the gooks were up to. Were they forming up to attack? There was an awful lot of them; they were all wandering around like lost sheep, having no idea what they should do. Then they ran away.

Ted got onto the set and told Marty what was going on. By that time, we had the top cover that Marty had brought in – Alouette IIIs in the form of a Cyclone 7 G-car trooper and a K-car. These two choppers had a better view up there of the running mass. We could hear the heavy cannon fire of the K-car and the machine guns on the trooper opening up as they identified moving targets.

We all felt a lot more secure with the helicopters above us. From the numbers, on observation, I could see from the high ground we now occupied that our group of twelve was heavily outnumbered. Then our call sign was detailed to move around behind the main ambush group onto the left flank, as far as the left-hand stop group position, then drop down into the riverbed, clearing the area from the left, through the killing ground and back to the right flank. Secure the killing ground and collect anything that Intel can use. In military parlance this is called the subsequent action, two words that give no idea or definition to just how dangerous the job is; this action had a set procedure to be followed. We were dropping down into the killing zone; I could see all kinds of twisted bodies when something went wrong. It was a brief, short exchange of fire. Ted was almost in the riverbed when I was dropped by three rounds, one smashing through my leg, and the other two into my body, putting me down. My partner was also hit, through his leg. We were both down. The next thing I know, the old sergeant from 22 SAS, Arthur (later lost at sea), was telling me to keep down as I was trying to sit up. Then I had medics sticking needles in me. I was shot three times and lived, my partner only once, and he died. Nothing can ever convey the genuine sadness of those left behind. A soldier is merely an ordinary person doing a job. Whether you like him or hate him, when he gets shot dead or blown to bits, someone will miss him, even if it's some hooker. We have military funerals and pomp and ceremony. That's not for the fallen soldier: he's in a box or what remains of him; they may have even put a sandbag or two in with him, so the coffin does not rattle. My teammate was the last of that family. He was the only child. His father had died some years before and his elderly mother spent her remaining years alone. Being a soldier can be fun, sometimes not so much.

The top cover was just on its Bingo line. That's when it has to break contact as it only has enough fuel to get home and can no longer loiter. I was dragged up to high ground by an Australian mate and two others. I was not a cooperative patient. I was cursing and swearing. I was waiting to pass out from my injuries, the half-severed leg bumping over every tree stump and clump of grass, but that relief just never came. I was entirely conscious and aware of everything going on. The chopper dropped down. I could hear the rotor blades slapping the tips of the trees. Having come in at such an angle due to the slope of the hill, if he made any mistake at all, he would have had to buy the air force a new aircraft. That or the blades would chop off our heads. Pulling and pushing they got the two of us into the chopper. There was no time for stretchers as the chopper was using a lot of avgas being in the hover position, and he was well on that Bingo line. He wanted to get off the ground, point his nose home and go or he was not going to get any of us out of there.

My partner had taken a nasty wound. He was bleeding, spraying all over, blood now blowing across the floor from the downdraft of the rotor blades. It ran a short distance down towards the open door where the gunner had sat but solidified before it could make its escape out over the edge. My leg was flapping around, the bones shattered, the lower part held in place by tissue and ligaments. I dragged it up and secured it to part of a bulkhead, to stop it from flapping around like a wet sheet on a washing line. I had no control over my legs at all. The door gunner was doing his best to keep my partner from bleeding out; the pilot was flying low and fast. All my little cobber and I could do was to lie there and try to stay alive. The pilot did a lot of dangerous flying to get us out. My mind was playing with me; all it kept on thinking was we're going down, we're going down, but the choppers kept on going. It would have been nice to pass out and wake up with it all over tucked up clean and safe in a hospital bed, but I willed myself to stay with it in case we did go down. My reality was a leg going flip-flop and banging against the floor of the chopper in the downdraft. The door gunner looked over to me to see how I was doing: there was not much bleeding from the leg after I had it positioned against the bulkhead. I gave him the okay. He went back to work to try and stop my mate's bleeding.

We landed at a remote bush airstrip. As good fortune would have it, or coincidence, a DC-3 'Dakota' was sitting on the dirt strip when our chopper put down. The Dak had been doing a training flight with a new pilot and had flown in to practise bush landings. We were now on stretchers. Medics worked to stabilize the two of us before being bundled on to the DC-3. I was promptly strapped to the floor. The skipper told the new flyer to move over as he was taking over. 'I want to get off the ground as soon as possible.' He stepped over me to get into the cockpit. The airstrip had no landing lights at all; it was an operational strip cut out of the bush. The pilot did his run-up and rotated off that strip when it was too dark even to see the end of it, assisted only by a Land Rover switching on its headlights.

We landed at New Sarum airbase in Salisbury and from there were taken by ambulance to Andrew Fleming Hospital in the middle of the city. We were wheeled in to casualty. We lay there for some time. I remember a crusty old SAS sergeant named Don, ex-Brit Paras, came in and removed my Rolex and other expensive bits of operational kit and personal items that I had on me. Knowing parachute soldiers as I do, I asked him if he was stealing my stuff and thought that the least he could do was wait until I was dead. Don told me he was going to keep it safe until I got out, so no one would nick it. That was encouraging: at least he thought I would be back. He was true to his word and I got everything returned later.

In casualty, everyone pretty much ignored me, other than to say 'The doctor's coming in.' They were working on my little mate next to me and I kept on wondering if they only had one doctor in the hospital. I was getting a little concerned about the service level. Also, I was beginning to feel. Not only had I been shot through the leg but also in the upper body. I had been on a drip for what felt like forever. They had not given me anything as I was going straight into theatre once the surgeon came in. Apart from what the medics had given me on site, I had had nothing else to ease the pain, and it was starting to wear off. I was getting to look a bit messy as the wounds were weeping through the field dressings. It's a kind of surreal world when you're lying there wondering if you're going to die, believing you are not going to even if you're bleeding and weeping out of holes punched in your body. Death happens to others but not you. My curly-haired little mate lay next to me, so close I could reach out and touch him, the same as in the ambush and on the chopper. He had stopped making any effort to talk to me some time ago; he was having trouble breathing. I think his lungs were collapsing. I watched them defibrillate him three times. Then my 20-year-old mate bled out next to me and died. They lifted me on to a trolley and wheeled me into the theatre.

There had been times throughout the ambush episode that I could have or should have died. I have seen some strange things in my time. A young parachute soldier goes through a farm gate that is booby-trapped with a 36 grenade; not only does he go through it once but he comes back through the same gate. He goes back and forward through it three times. The trip does not trip, the pin is out but the spoon stays in place. Whenever I went into an ambush site or to ground, I would drape what is called a scrim net or face veil over my head; it's like the scarves issued to soldiers in the Parachute Regiment. When you drape it over your head, it breaks up your shape as it falls from your head down around your shoulders. For a simple metre-square piece of camouflaged lightweight netting, it's tremendously useful. I have had a gook almost walk over me and not be aware I was that close. When Ted moved us up to the high ground, I had my face veil over my head. Marty had hooked around the back of us to have a look at what was happening on the flank. He saw me moving and thought I was enemy as all he could see was this unidentifiable camouflaged thing running where his stop group was. He told me later he was already aiming to drop me with a headshot when I pulled off my face veil as it was sweltering running up that slope trying to breathe through the netting. Once the scrim was off, all Marty had in his sights was this blond head, mine. Gooks don't do blond hair. I was milliseconds from being dispatched with a headshot.

Then all of a sudden, I had this older man bending over me saying he was Dr Nangle. He said it as if I should have known him. I didn't have a clue who he was. I told him, 'I don't come here often so we wouldn't have met.' A little light humour helps in such situations. He was wearing an Airborne Forces regimental tie, which cheered me up a little. I asked him if they had they flown him in from England as I had been waiting for some time. No, he had been to the Airborne regimental do – 'drink-e-dos with the chaps'. They'd had to find him. We had a 'little chat' as he called it so the two of us could get to know one another and he would have more of an idea on whom he was going operate. He wanted to know what had happened. Considering the circumstances, he was charming, friendly and chatty, with a pleasant bedside manner. That's when I started to think I was going to be okay – he was Airborne. Strange as it may sound, special forces and airborne troops do have a bond: we have built-in confidence that we can depend on one another. I told him I was 2 Para before SAS and could he try not to cut off the leg as I didn't think they allowed one-legged parachute soldiers. We both agreed I would try and stay alive; he would look after the leg. He told me he had 'looked after plenty of you chaps up in North Africa in the last show'. Then 'See you in surgery' and off he went.

The medical team brought in were the best the world had to offer at that time. Mr Nangle had been putting soldiers back together since the Second World War and was still doing it when I showed up. I was fortunate that two doctors, both highly skilled in their area of medical expertise and speciality, were on call that night. One worked on my stomach as the other put my leg back together. Two rounds had clipped my lower spine then bounced off. I would, fortunately, not spend the rest of my life in a wheelchair. One round had torn up some of my insides before lodging in a muscle, while the other ended up in my pelvic cavity. I never did meet the miracle workers as I was already asleep on the table. Nangle was good to his word, and I got to keep my leg, and everything was put back in the right place inside my insides by Mr Standish-White.

Another miracle was that the hospital had just taken possession of a new kind of X-ray machine. Technically, I don't know much about how it worked, other than what they told me later. The images of the damage were in real-time, so instead of cutting my leg open to get to the bone and set it or amputate, Nangle just kneaded the bones and managed to move the bits that were in the leg until they were close enough to grow back together. He never put pins or a plate in and the bones over time knitted. Having bone marrow shattered and splashed around inside a young person is dangerous as bone marrow is highly toxic and can cause death, even when in the short term you look as if you're recovering. Some months before a Special Air Service soldier had stepped on an anti-personnel mine. He suffered a small wound to his heel and up to his leg. The heel bone shattered in his foot; the injury should have healed within weeks. However, it did not, and he died from the toxicity of the bone marrow entering the bloodstream only days later. I think it is called toxaemia. I had bone fragments all around a wound area so large you could have put two fists into it but no toxaemia. I lived.

I was in a ward with two other wounded. One had a similar leg wound – same area same leg; he got hit in a vehicle ambush. The bullet went straight through without damaging the bone, but the doctors were having a difficult time battling the infection. I never had any infection whatsoever.

What I did have one morning was a little bit of pure white cotton wool in my bed. I wondered if it had come out the top of the plaster cast. I went to brush it away and it moved. I could not believe it, so I picked the thing up, whatever it was, and put it on my bedside table and just watched it. It started to move. I called a nurse who did not believe me, so she watched too. Yep! It wiggled, so she went and called the matron, who in turn thought I was messing with them. After it moved for the matron, she went and brought back someone in a white coat and a specimen jar who dropped the little living ball of pure white cotton wool that had a life of its own into the pot, and off they went. Nangle had gone off fishing for a few days. Honestly, he put me back together, watched me for a day or two then off he went fishing. Before he left, he came to see my leg, saying he was 'going fishing, back in a day or so'. I found the little white ball of fluff had mates coming out the top of the plaster cast. The specialist's understudy convinced me he knew what was going on. So, what was the loose ball of fluff? They were what are called sterile maggots. I know, very distasteful, but true. Repugnant as it may sound, the dead flesh on the wound had been eaten and the little buggers were on the move looking for food which was why they were coming out the top of my plaster cast. To clean out the wound, they cut a window in the plaster cast to wash out whatever was in there. Then they closed the aperture. Somehow, and no one was talking, I had sterile maggots in the wound area, the crème de la crème of the maggot world with no nastiness in them: they are not carriers of germs or transporters of parasites. I don't think they can even reproduce outside of a laboratory. The only treatment from then on was that my wound was douched out with peroxide once a day and still, no one was talking. I believe this technique was common in the First World War. I have no real proof of such, but the story was revealed to me by a medic weeks later.

Another wounded in the ward was up and walking within two or three days and was doing well. He even came over to me and we had a chat. Then something went wrong with his gut wound and he died one night, after looking as if he would be okay. I was not the happiest person in the world, but on the other hand, had healed abnormally fast and was alive. I was moved out of critical care and into another ward that was for those who'd live.

After training hard, I went back on ops, but to say I was the same would be stretching the imagination. I returned to the squadron and did what was called soft ops to try and get back into it. However, things were not going well. I did a reconnaissance patrol into Porkers with an old cobber of mine from Australia. After that op, he called me November Whisky (nervous worry).

Later I was involved in a first-class waterborne operation. We were to do a crossing into Zambia by boat at night. We had a motor launch on loan from the Fisheries Department. We were the tugboat for a team that was going to use two-man canoes to paddle into a target. The Rhodesian Army did not have submarines so we went for the tugboat option; we had four or five Klepper canoes in tow. Our task, once we had dropped the teams, was to move out into the lake and loiter on standby, as back-up if they got into difficulty. Lake Kariba is the size of a small sea. There was no moon and no stars were out, so it was very dark. Midway across the lake, before target and before we cut away the teams, we bumped into a large group of terrorists in a small flotilla of boats, clearly crossing the lake to infiltrate Rhodesia; they mistook us for civilian day-trippers lost on the lake after dark, trying to get back to safety on the Rhodesian side. We sent up flares and caught the entire group of boats in the open. They had no place to hide and could not outrun, outsail or outswim us. They had no option but to fight. They did try. Streams of green tracer came in high and hit the transom board at the back of the bridge that was carrying two spare outboard motors used for the lifeboat that we did not have. Both outboards came crashing down and fell on me. The firefights went on as long as we had light from the flares but once they fell into the lake, they went out and, in the darkness, we lost the targets. Then we put up more illumination but they had made a run for it. Our boat was driven by two powerful marine diesel engines and there was no way that they could escape. The action would start up again every time a flare went up. We expended thousands of rounds of ammunition; rumour was we shot off about 40,000 rounds, both rifle and belt-fed as we put down withering and continuous volleys of fire. Every time we illuminated the gooks with a flare, we opened up. Once on target, no one stopped firing until darkness once more enveloped the enemy, giving them cover. No fire control, no watch and shoot, just pop and chop before it goes dark. We still had the raider teams on board so there were plenty of people shooting. Our outgoing firepower was catastrophic for the enemy. Once the firefight had stopped, we pulled the enemy boats alongside the launch to retrieve their backpacks, for intelligence and maps. All their craft were burning. We counted thirteen bodies at the bottom of one boat alone. We had to cut one loose when we saw rows of landmines lying in the bottom of the hull, and it was burning. All in all, there must have been about five or six boats shot up and burning, each with around a dozen bodies in. There were no survivors.

After that my life in the SAS started to become more complicated. There was some talk of me not getting my para pay and other allowances. My relationship with the married woman I was living with was not going well either. I was suffering from a massive personality shift, and all I wanted to do was get back into the bush on ops and into a comfortable call sign, where I would not have to explain anything and just soldier.

I was not operating at the same level of efficiency as I had been before being wounded. I no longer had a job and was handed menial tasks to do. I would also from time to time wander off, going to the movies in the afternoon or just sitting in some little bistro having coffee. All this without bothering that I had left my place of duty or forgetting just what it was I was meant to be doing. Being a foreign soldier, I had no family, and the military at that time had not established a safe house for wounded troops, to get them out the way. So, I had no place to go and nothing to do but hang around, limping to coffee shops

In any highly operational unit, teams and call signs change, people move on, get killed or get promoted. I was getting left behind. One operator that I had soldiered with was Scotty (USMC) who would talk to himself, something he did often, calling himself 'Scotty baby'. He suggested I had made 'a big mistake'.

'Rob, you lived, you're an embarrassment, limping around; we are not meant to get wounded and live. You remind them things can go wrong fast.'

Time passed and I did more soft ops – reconnaissance or observation posts, mine-laying. I agreed that if things went wrong, I would dump and run so, when the team bugged out, I would move away in another direction. It would be impossible for me to keep up with them if they had to bug out fast. At least they were letting me soldier; maybe I would come right.

I was still living with my married lady; she used to get up early and be out of the house every Sunday to go to dog training. I think she did this to get away from me. I was never violent, but I had morphed into someone else. I did not hear voices in my head. I was not psychotic. I did not have a head wound. I did go back into the bush and my war. Wouldn't this be a beautiful story if I was to tell you the sun came out and the whole world was rosy and my life improved and I got what I had wished for, accompanied by music, sunshine and marshmallows? I don't think so and the wheels started to fall off. I was in a dark place. What she had seen as endearing now became unbearable. Then the 'you're starting to worry me' talk.

By 1975, I was back on operations with A Troop, C Squadron SAS. I was on an op with John, the Australian mate of mine who had helped to get me into the casevac chopper. Whenever I said I don't like this or that doesn't feel good, he used to tell me, 'You just got to get back into it, mate. She'll be right, mate. You just need a couple of good contacts, and then you're over it.' I don't remember how far we were inside Porkers when John opened a small can of food then threw the empty tin in the bush. I told him that's not who we were, that we had both trained in the Australian Army. If someone found the tin, we'd have a company of gooks on us. I was hyper, hypersensitive.

In August of that year, I was part of a sizeable vehicle-mounted attack into Mozambique. I was on a vehicle with Big John, later killed on HALO (High Altitude Low Opening) freefall, an officer and a gentleman in the genuine sense of the word. He had served previously with the US Army Airborne, before coming to join C squadron. Also on the vehicle was Clandestine Clive (later KIA) who had served first in the Royal Marines and then with the Australian SAS, before coming across to the Rhodesian SAS. Last but not least was USMC Scotty Baby. I don't recall the driver of the vehicle.

The convoy was strategically loaded one team to a fighting vehicle. We were coming back through a region called the Honde Valley, which was a very active area. My team must have been about the thirteenth or fourteenth vehicle in the convoy. Each fighting vehicle was mine-proofed with rows of sandbags layered on the vehicle bed, the bags then covered with conveyor belting. It had shown itself to be able to take considerable blasts from a landmine even when boosted. Mine casualties had been reduced considerably using this technique.

When we hit the mine, all four of us went about fifteen feet up in the air. Enveloped in a thick cloud of dust, we were deposited like rag dolls into the bush at the side of the road. Clive was unconscious and lying in a strange twisted shape and looked as if he was dead but was not. Scotty was next to me looking for his rifle and John was trying to organize us into all-around defensive for what he thought would be an incoming assault but was incoherent with shock. I still had a death-like grip on my rifle but had no feeling in my legs, and I thought my back had been shot out. Having been punched off that vehicle with such force, I thought a 12.7 round had hit me in the centre of my back. The blast had come up through a gap in the mine-proofing. The concussion from the explosion hit slap-bang on my not-so-old wounds. Having been shot before with rounds clipping my spine, I was paranoid about being back-shot and never walking again.

The first person to get to me was Mulligan, an ex-Royal Marine. I kept on telling him they had shot my back out. I was in total shock. Only after Mulligan ran his hands under my webbing and along my back and showed me there was no blood, did I get a grip and settle down before getting the feeling back into my legs. It took us hours to get a casevac to a hospital in the border town of Umtali. The four of us were not injured enough to warrant a chopper. It was just a landmine incident; there are lots of them; sort it out and get on with the job: no top cover, no air support. I had a concussion as did everyone and shrapnel wounds as did everyone who came off the back of that truck. It took over six hours to get to the Umtali hospital. Though only slightly wounded, six hours on a vehicle was a long time to travel, especially at night. I felt like everyone in the world was trying to kill me. It was very personal as I lay on the truck, knowing full well that we might be hit again. It was just not doing it for me. Being blown up was more traumatic than the first time I was wounded and it was the beginning of the end for me as an operator in the SAS.

I got back okay but was a little confused. Here I was almost getting killed again: lightning does not strike in the same place twice, or does it? The war carried on, as did I, but I was taking strain. It was 0230 hours. I remember the time as I looked at my watch. I was lying in bed with my woman who was 'starting to worry'. I knew she was also awake by her breathing. She was not looking at the ceiling like me but I could tell she was not sleeping either. She asked what was wrong and why was I awake at that ridiculous hour: she had to work in the morning. The tension in the room was real, almost tangible; the only words that came out my mouth as I lay next to her were, 'Christ, I'm scared of getting back on those fighting vehicles!' Was it a prayer, a call for help or blasphemy? She cried herself to sleep next to me. Our relationship came to an end a short time later, ultimately her wondering who would get killed next: me, or some other we knew. It all became too much for her. The end came when she was watching TV and the military issued a security force communiqué: there were names of people we both knew killed that day on an operation, somewhere. All she said to me was, 'Yes! You people don't believe you can die.' She moved out a short time later.

I thought about moving back into camp. I was still operational. I remember sitting on a vehicle when Jock, a pal of mine from the Brit Paras, came and took all his kit off the truck. I thought the op had been cancelled.

I asked, 'Are we stood down?'

'No,' he replied, 'but I am not getting on a truck near you, mate; you're a magnet for hot lead.'

In November I was wandering along in my little world as I would from time to time when the medical officer, a doctor from New

Zealand, walked over to me and asked how I was coping: was I all right? A simple inquiry. I told him I had some slight concerns about ops, what I jokingly called a healthy anxiety, but would get over it.

The next sentence out of his mouth was, 'Get your medical documents, Rob; you're being boarded out.' It was said quietly, I think with compassion or sadness at the situation, not only mine but the country and the people in general.

I went to see a doctor in the Medical Corps, a colonel or brigadier. I handed him a file. It had very little in it. He examined me, noted the scar tissue on my body, called in a sergeant and asked him why in the blue blazes was this man still in the army? I should have been out months ago. It took about four weeks for me to be medically discharged.

In 1978, the adjutant Mick asked me if I'd go back onto active duty. They had just had some vote and had elected Abel Muzorewa as the first black prime minister of Rhodesia, or Zimbabwe-Rhodesia as it became, and whom the international community had rejected out of hand. I refused. I walked away. I never went back or fought again in that war.

My service record with the Rhodesian Special Air Service shows I served two years and ninety days (excluding the two six-week call-ups I did in 1977 and 1978). In that time, I had been wounded twice, three times if you count the two outboard motors falling on me. The first time badly, the second time not so much, but psychologically the second time was worse. Scotty Baby was right: 'Rob you should have died,' but I didn't and maybe it was just another coincidence. One morning it dawned on me that I had no girlfriend, no job and little prospects for the future, with a genuine possibility that sometime soon, I would have no place to live.

As one war ends, as they all do, another is smouldering. I was recruited by the South African Defence Force, as was most of the Rhodesian Special Air Service on the conclusion of the Rhodesian conflict – when the country became Zimbabwe under Robert Mugabe in April 1980. I crossed into South Africa in November 1980 and went straight to 6 Reconnaissance Commando. On completion of my contract, I left the SADF. I wandered around for a time but found it difficult to adjust to civilian life or living in the real world.

There are different kinds of people in the world, and likewise, there are different kinds of people who become soldiers. You can conscript a young man and make him a soldier. He will hate you, detest the military and can't get out of it soon enough. He is usually bitter and resentful of his time spent, seeing it as wasted years. He will adjust back into civilian life, but not well, and for a period loathe what he was part of. This period of his life haunts him for a considerable time. In today's lexicon, it is called PTSD. Then you have the full-term lifer who will spend his whole career in the same military unit. He may never see combat or active service. That is not his job. He may be a mechanic, a cook or any one of a hundred jobs in the military. He is no less critical and is every bit as essential as the frontline soldier. The army or any branch of the service where he serves would have a difficult time functioning without him. He will do his twenty years, retire with a pension and then tell war stories in his old age at the bar. You also get the hard-core professional, or to quote one journalist 'the flotsam and jetsam left behind after every war ends'. This person can't stay in a peacetime army. He moves on; it's pointless being in a military that does not fight. It is what he is, what he has been trained for; he has become an adrenaline junky. He is usually not a big man and looks like an average person, young or old, father, brother or husband, if he is lucky enough to stay married. Although scared out of his mind from time to time, the buzz he needs is found only in war. Does he have PTSD? In all probability yes, but he does not believe there is such a thing. Life for him is split up into time frames that consist of 95 per cent waiting/ boredom and 5 per cent abject terror. I found it impossible to settle. By 1983, I was looking for ways to get back into the loop. I need this: I am a soldier.

I received a letter from the South African military within a short space of time, in fact, only days. It had my number, rank and name and one line: 'The SADF no longer requires your services.' Three years later I would be headhunted by Military Intelligence for Psychological Operations (PsyOps) and other projects. It would turn out to be the job of a lifetime – what the Americans call black ops. I would once more work in a world that did not exist, and all done with smoke and mirrors: I was to work for CSI (Chief of Staff Intelligence) for six years.

Chapter 6

South Africa, Special Forces, Black Ops and I Spy

'I don't know what you mean by "glory",' Alice said.

Humpty Dumpty smiled contemptuously. 'Of course you don't –
till I tell you. I meant "there's a nice knock-down argument for
you!"'

'But "glory" doesn't mean "a nice knock-down argument",' Alice
objected.

'When I use a word,' Humpty Dumpty said, in rather a scornful
tone, 'it means just what I choose it to mean – neither more nor
less.'

Lewis Carroll, *Alice Through the Looking Glass*

The Rhodesian SAS had moved en masse down to South
Africa at the end of the bush war. I entered South
Africa on 11 November 1980, going to 6 Reconnaissance
Commando on the Bluff, in Durban. I signed a short-term contract
as did many of the older soldiers from the Rhodesia conflict. Some
went to 32 'Buffalo' Battalion, others to the Cape and joining the
'Crayfish Recces' (divers and little boats). Dribs and drabs from the
SAS ended up all over South Africa in different units at the end of
play in Rhodesia. We became displaced people.

Sometime shortly before the Rhodesian conflict came to its
disastrous conclusion, and before exiting the fray, a close friend of
mine, Ian, visited me at home. He presented me with a possibility,
or a cockamamie idea subject to how one looked at the world, about

a soldiering job. The talk was of an island and an operation that would pay good money. The raid would only last about seventy-two hours. He could only give me limited information. I asked him what our exfiltrate was, in other words: how do we get back out, and, if it's an island, how far would we have to swim? Ian's reticence seemed strange as I knew him as a good soldier who had, before joining the SAS, served as a Royal Marine, or as he would say 'the Real Marines'. Ian was killed on an external operation working with a recce team before this job came to fruition. I heard nothing more about the operation until I had been in South Africa for some time.

To say it was an unhappy marriage between the Rhodesians and the South Africans would be one of the world's understatements. It was a relationship that went sour from the start; the acrimony ran deep. I spent most of my time trying to get paid. For the first six weeks, I lived in a hotel in Durban and travelled to the Bluff on a military bus, being paid out of what I assumed were regimental funds. Many of us had to live in hotels due to a shortage of billeting. One of the consequences of hotel living was being unable to cook in your room: we ate at the hotel restaurants – a costly affair. However, the military refused to cover our messing costs; they only paid for accommodation, not meals out, their view being there was food at the camp, so we were meant to eat at the base then return to the hotel to sleep. The problem was feeding the families.

I then had to fight for my parachute pay; also, to be allowed to put my wings and ribbons on my uniform. I had done three para courses with three different Special Forces units, and I had an imbecile who had wounded himself when playing with some explosives telling me I could not wear wings. His whole attitude was insulting not only to me personally but to the Rhodesians as a whole; we were a defeated people. Once I overcame this appalling stance, I spoke with a major who knew the people in the parachute training school in the UK and he verified the signatures on my freefall documents. I never did put on my freefall wings as I could see it was going to create problems. The only thing they did get right was my upgraded rank for more money. When I was recruited in Rhodesia, the South Africans had promised that my pay scale would be substantial. Fortunately, I had this in writing.

The reality was the South African Defence Force had a dual language policy. It was a bilingual army. One day officially they would speak Afrikaans the next day English, and no one gave a toss if you could not speak English. They were protective of their language and culture in many respects, fearful of being anglicized. With all this, I was still willing to soldier.

The final blow for many good Rhodesian soldiers was when an operator got killed on a raid in Mozambique. Some of his specialized equipment went missing, as is inevitable when an operator gets killed, and the South African Army, when paying out the final salary to his widow, deducted money for the missing equipment. Everyone personally felt the injustice. At that time, the South Africans believed they did not need the rest of the world or anyone outside of their cultural bubble; many were still fighting the Anglo-Boer War that ended in 1902. Some Afrikaners still believe they are the only nation that ever suffered in a war.

Some years later, when I came back to serve in the South African military after completion of my first contract, the war had progressed somewhat and attitudes had mellowed. They knew they were in for a difficult time even though militarily they were unmatched on the African continent. Put bluntly, they knew they were heading for shit. South Africa needed all the friends it could get.

My first impression of the Afrikaners was that they were very Teutonic and Calvinistic with a basic slapstick, custard-pie humour. In contrast, the Anglo humour is very dry, caustic and with a quick, subtle wit, holding very little reverence for anyone or anything. Culturally, though, we were different, due mostly to South Africa's history and international isolation. The English-speaking soldier can from time to time drive the Ruperts to distraction, almost to the point of tears, especially those not in the SAS.

I would not have the audacity to say South Africa's Special Forces were not highly trained and excellent: their performance was brilliant in every regard. The young men of the Reconnaissance Regiment were fearless in battle, accomplishing successes far beyond their numerical size. The SADF never lost a battle. They fought for the survival of their country. That they, along with other civilized peoples of South Africa, were sacrificed on the altar of political expediency by their leaders, is now written into history – people who got enough money to spend the rest of their lives on some sunbaked island is no reflection on the Reconnaissance troops. They were loyal, brave and dedicated then betrayed and sold down the river. There was nowhere in Africa they would not go in pursuit of the enemy. Special forces produced some incredibly daring young men who performed magnificently against all the odds. The Rhodesian SAS soldiers who stayed with the South African Special Force became very much part of the Recce success story. In reality, the South Africans did not need the handful of Rhodesians that migrated south at the end of the Rhodesian war. They did us a favour. Many Rhodesians, who were war-weary after completing their contracts, used South Africa as a waypoint or springboard, moving on and making their homes in new countries such as Australia New Zealand, North America and Europe. I think I was every bit as fatigued as the rest.

I don't recall the actual date that I went to work for the Chief of Staff Intelligence. It was rumoured, due to my Laos involvement, that I was CIA – something people became aware of in the late 1970s due to another operator, Clive, who had been a member of both the Royal Marines and the Australian SAS in Vietnam. Clive formulated this opinion after talking with me when we were together in hospital after being wounded. Another time people thought that owing to my covert work with the MRF in Northern Ireland, I was MI6 or any one of the numerous alphabet soup agencies. All this speculation hindered my job prospects from time to time.

South Africa was to become a hotbed of intrigue, unconventional and covert operations, deceit, code names, and spy versus spy, hitmen, murders and assassinations. The number of mercenary groups and coup d'états that were planned at the La Parisienne café in Hillbrow, downtown Johannesburg, would in all probability be too many to document. A little like Laos.

South Africa had always been a divided country. I relate to my involvement with them only from the time I entered in 1980 until the 1990s. I had completed my short-term contract with the SADF in 1981. After being a civilian for a short time, I was approached once more about the 'Island Job' (the Seychelles) that was supposedly clouded in secrecy. Still, everyone knew something was on and had knowledge about Operation Anvil. Ian had been killed on an external operation as mentioned and I had moved on. When the venture came around once more, I was already on another paying task. That excluded me from the offer of the Seychelles adventure. I, in my folly, had shown an interest in doing Anvil, irrespective of having been strongly advised against it due to its shortcomings and the genuine possibility of failure. Sometime earlier, a top South African soldier, after perusal of their planning, had warned me that the Island Job would in all probability be a total disaster: 'So don't get involved.' Poorly conceived, deficient in preparation and, as history proved, unsatisfactorily executed, Operation Anvil was just that, a disaster. The sums of money mentioned were plentiful, amounts of money that at the end of the day did not materialize, leading to many operators going broke and losing everything they had.

Contrary to belief, Operation Anvil was not the only attempt against the Seychelles. I later met a gentleman called 'The Commodore' from the South African Institute for Maritime Research (SAIMR) that supposedly had close links to MI6. The Commodore confirmed this, and through a short history and background briefing provided at La Parisienne, it was more than just implied. One could form an opinion that it had a working relationship with the American CIA, as well as the Israeli Mossad. It had been suggested by those who circled the periphery of such groups – NGOs and people looking for fame by association – that our unknown Commodore, Keith Maxwell, was a charlatan and quack of some kind. Although, in doing my due diligence on him, I found SAIMR to be who they said they were.

Keith put forward some superb operational plans for successful undertakings. To me, it highlighted that the man and the organization were far more than perceived. Had his plan been used for Anvil, it would have been a success. It was a sound concept. South Africans could be extremely insular at times and I think this is why it was passed over, due to his dealings with outside agencies. The stories about SAIMR held some truth, but most reports were creative spin. The only person who knows the full history of SAIMR is Maxwell, and no one knows where he is today. Indeed, was his name even Maxwell? Our tracks would cross from time to time, without any actual contact, a bit like footprints in the snow. After the South African government capitulated to the communist ANC, I never had contact with him again; I did not need to: the success of undercover operations is gauged by what people don't know and never find out.

There had been some talk of me going to Angola for Military Intelligence. I had even done interviews for the job and wanted it. The recruiter came back and explained, with some regret, that his particular branch was unable to use me as they were only taking people with some form of a degree (read the *Volk*, the Afrikaans people). As already stated, at times my history got in the way of employment.

Purely out of interest, one evening, I went to a political meeting of what I term the great white unwashed, or useful idiots as the Soviets called them. One after another of the speakers was attacking the South African Defence Force. To start, it did not bother me overly much; it was not my army, was it? then they began to do a hatchet job on soldiers A mother told how the army had turned her son into an alcoholic. I always thought one came out with what you went in with, or better, unless of course, you had bits shot or blown off. The military can only work with what it's given. A young man related how he had done national service, lambasting the army and telling some awful horror stories, all being patently untrue. He was sucking up all the attention, people hanging on his every word. I know operational soldiers, and this was not one of them: he was a tasteless, weak, uninspiring person, a degenerate little wannabe, most certainly no combat veteran. He went on and on to reveal unspeakable horrors about the military and its dastardly deeds. It got worse in the telling. I just thought enough already. Life is about choices: I could walk out and ignore this absolute nonsense, go home have something to eat then go to bed, or I could draw my Colt .45 and shoot him in the head. At that distance, there was a possibility I would miss and kill the old lady sharing the platform with him, but hit or miss I would have spent a long time behind bars.

When Military Intelligence first approached me, my simple question was, 'Why me?' They had a whole host of highly qualified people in the military. I was a rare combination, so I was told, based on the following: I was a Christian, so I would be comfortable circulating within church environs. And having been in the military, I understood the military culture, and why at times they do things for no apparent reason, that to a civilian would seem outlandish. Plus, I held two legally obtained passports. To top it all, as the general was to say, using a misquote: 'Rob, a prophet is not listened to in his own country. You speak with a different accent, come from a different country and have been involved in the fight against terrorists overseas, meaning people will think you know something they don't.' There it was: I was an expert.

At first, I was a little sceptical. Would I be able to do the job? Did I want this kind of soldiering? Would it be tedious at best and pointless at worst? Not having the proverbial crystal ball, I did not know. I was unaware that I was entering into one of the most interesting, exciting, educational and, at times, most dangerous six years of my life. Once again, I would see intelligence organizations mutate from intelligence-gathering to the capacity to wage war. As I progressed and became more established and immersed in my new world of smoke and mirrors, I was to meet and work with fantastic people who, simply put, had brilliant minds and were forward thinkers. They understood geopolitics more than most politicians and had no delusions as to South Africa's fate and what awaited her people should they not win. They have been proved correct in all their assumptions. They were not starry-eyed about the future. Each person I worked with fought the good fight in their unique way, against the liberal left and the Marxist Utopian New World Order. They were neither racists nor bigots: they were researchers, academics and brilliant analysts. I was close to both Christians and non-believers, as well as the military personnel with whom I operated and worked alongside. We all had one common goal: to try and save South Africa from the horrors seen in the rest of Africa; trying to stop South Africa from getting into the awful state where it is now. Before entering this phase of the war, I had thought the battle was against evil little men in straw hats and black pyjamas, or the masked faces of IRA bombers, along with the viciousness of AK-wielding terrorists in the Rhodesian bush when they burned African huts and mutilated people mostly from their own ethnic group. I had seen the sharp, double-edged blade of terrorism.

The war I was to become involved in had no uniforms, no medal parades, no bands, no pomp and no ceremony. Operators would disappear and if lucky found held in some African jail; others would just no longer exist. As a close friend and fellow Australian operator once told me: 'Rob, if we are found dead in the gutter with our head run over by a truck, not too many people are going to be looking for the truck driver.' Such was the world I operated in. Years later,

I was to contact a retired general, a former head of SADF Military Intelligence. His question to me was, 'Rob, how did you disappear so quickly and completely that no one could get hold of you or knew where you had gone?' After I had hung up the phone, I dwelled on his question: my response – I am a professional, trained to do so and my services were no longer required.

Many of the people I organized or who organized me have moved on, some to other countries; many would, in all probability, have families and a new life. For this reason, I mention only one, a first-class woman in every sense of the word. I don't know how I met Aida Parker, but I did. Aida was born in 1918 in the south of England. I don't know when she took up residence in South Africa but once, when I was privileged to have lunch with her, she pointed out I was eating off the very plates that Lord Kitchener had eaten off when he had visited her family home; where that was I had no idea. I did know in her early years Aida had been a rabid communist and had travelled to the Soviet Union but became disenchanted and left sometime later. I also believe she was one of the first journalists to enter Angola after the country had been invaded by Holden Roberto's FNLA (National Front for the Liberation of Angola) terrorist gangs in the early 1960s. Aida would also tell me of the rich and famous people she had met over the years. She was, without doubt, one of the most exciting and mentally stimulating women I ever met. She was not young when I met her. Aida was connected to many of the world's influential people, not only in the world of espionage but also academia. Whenever revealing something about a person she knew, she would shrug her shoulders, her eyes would squint almost closed and then she'd smile or laugh much like a naughty little girl telling tales; she'd tell me not to tell anyone, saying, 'I will get into the most awful trouble.' She also had the habit of licking her fingertips, I think because of dry skin from typing on an old typewriter, or maybe she did not like the feel of paper. She also had dyslexia. Then there was a gentleman friend of hers, a Deputy Director of the CIA in one administration, one of America's legendary intelligence officers, especially during the Vietnam War; his name popped into her head when she asked me about Laos. She would reel off names of authors she knew personally and told me I should read their books. Towards the end, the Aida Parker newsletter had to set up its own legal defence fund. Her newsletter must have been hurting the ANC/SACP as well as the National Party as it tried to play the pied piper and lead the people of South Africa into a new future under the communists. The newsletter was the subject of unremitting legal terrorism from the radicals. Politically motivated lawsuits that were baseless and with no merit at all were churned out like proverbial sausages from a machine with no possibility of success but Aida was incurring hefty legal expenses. All this wasted time, along with the mental stress all designed to keep her from using her poison pen, almost worked, but not quite. The National Party was determined to sell South Africa out with obscene haste. Different organizations that we ran had been the bulwark against an encroaching evil; now the barbarians where at the gates, then overnight, my organization and others came under surveillance. We were personally threatened, attacked, investigated, spied on and subjected to electronic monitoring from the very people we were working for and helping. We were now the enemy, and short of a coup, the military was limited in its actions. Many people took the credit when I was released from an African prison and for getting the team out. A little-known truth never made public was Aida Parker, through her contacts, got us out. Let's say I am not easily impressed. Let's say she knew a man who knew another man who was once in the Royal Navy who married well. In a word, Aida did know people, the right kind of people. The last word of who she was and what she thought must go to Aida herself: 'There are, unfortunately, no precedents to point the way for a people who no longer accept any definition of right or wrong, whose governing and educational bodies reject the idea of excellence, who place a pathological emphasis on so-called egalitarianism.'* In February 2003, Aida died, and much of what she predicted for South Africa has come to pass. Her predictions today are being played out. She was accurate through her brilliant research and analysis. I wish she had not been. I lost a dear friend.

My line function was vast, and there was never any shortage of funds. The South African military was the best army on the African continent. When it came to covert ops and the propaganda war, I was soon to find out the South Africans compared with other people I had worked for, were somewhat brutish. Not a lot of subtlety there. When I set up my organization, it was to recruit and run other agents, operators and NGOs. Intelligence was awash with money, and they wanted to give lots and lots of it to me. They had assessed my needs and figured that if I were to be successful in my role, I would require all kinds of new toys. I did, however, point out to them that if I had a rapid inflow of money and a new car and lots of new toys, then should we be successful in the future, people would pick up on this instant wealth. The first thing they would do was follow the money, so best not make me rich overnight. I opted for a little second-hand vehicle, and a dingy office in a seedy part of town that doubled as my place of abode. All my equipment was second hand, and there was not very much of that either, but it was a start. I opened a string of post boxes to facilitate operations and involvement with cross-border ops. I even went overseas for another section on three occasions. My brief was broad: I was to establish various counter groups that would work or obstruct and yes, the word 'destroy' was used in my brief relating to anything or person that was supportive of the ANC. My targets were plentiful, from an organization that propagated and encouraged young men not to do military service, to covert operations outside the country.

---

* Associated Press.

The End Conscription Campaign was a worry until we infiltrated it and got people inside on the ground. The military had visions of anti-war demos much the same as the anti-Vietnam War demos in the US. The ECC had little influence or success and no role in the ending of apartheid. We let them run rather than close them down and have something new pop up that we did not know about, and where we'd have to start all over again. What success they did have was mostly among English speakers and left-wing conscientious objectors, but they were still working for me.

My role was multifaceted, including training, intelligence-gathering and local and trans-border operations. I was busy with members of private organizations and NGOs that were beneficial to the military, but who did not work for it. I was to keep them out of trouble, as sometimes in their enthusiasm and anti-communist/anti-ANC verve, they would land themselves in mortal danger. They were more use to us as civilians and alive rather than dead or languishing in some jail in darkest Africa.

The SADF faced several challenges, a major one being they were restricted in their movements using South African passports. They were able and capable of mounting military operations to almost any point of the compass and at any distance. Still, they had a significant problem with covert work and intelligence-gathering not only inside South Africa but also trans-border. For all the world's hi-tech equipment, the best intel you can get is still from an intelligence operator who has boots on the ground or is unobtrusively seen as your enemy. If one is facing opposition in any given area of operation, then logically, the 'best' resistance you can face is that created by yourself. You can then organize and control it. People who wish to get involved and fight against your principles are what we call joiners or willing workers as they want to do something. They would find a welcoming home in your newly formed bogus opposition group. Creating one's own opposition has many advantages. For starters, you will know who they are, you know what they believe, what they are willing to do to try and stop you, how they perceive your operation. They may even tell you what would have been more effective against them. They can be used unwittingly for false flag actions and operations. They may also contribute financially and you can then use their money for your real activities – to destroy their organization. Once established, your fake do-good–feel-good group will become a regular part of the opposition. In time, you will be invited to take part in other group activities and closed meetings, and all this information will, of course, end up on a desk run by someone like me, sitting atop an in-tray labelled INTELLIGENCE OF OPPOSING STRUCTURES with names, dates and function. The moral of the story: don't join anything unless you know who runs it and for what end. People like to talk; to be a good operator all you have to do is listen. The average person has no idea the amount of intelligence gathered from reading newspapers, magazines, books and media statements, reading other people's mail or listening to pillow talk. It's even easier today with the internet. I had a whole team of people working as cutters; each one would be given a particular topic, personality or media outlet. Along with other means, we would build up a history and profile. Mr and Mrs Average have no idea just how disgusting many leadership personalities are. A lot of the information we captured and files we built up were later taken and destroyed. When asked why, after our operators had put themselves in harm's way, was the information being spiked or erased, the powers that be would say it 'unbalanced the political arena ... we have to have someone to talk to'.

Military Intelligence had, for some time, been brainstorming to find solutions to problems that had not appeared to be problems a short time before. The second National Consultative Conference held in 1985 at Kabwe in Zambia – a hostile African country north of the Zambezi – set up a department of religious affairs that was mandated to initiate active participation of the Christian community, through class consciousness, politicization and guilt manipulation, to become active for what they termed a new

Democratic South Africa. That was, in reality, a communist South Africa that would be forced on the people, and achieved through propaganda, liberation theology and the concept of an unjust war. It was a new problem for the South African Defence Force that they had not seen coming down the track and it blindsided them. They thought all they had to do was fight and kill enough ANC cadres in Angola or anywhere else they found them, including Europe, and *voila*! Problem solved. The South Africans now faced the possibility that churches would be hijacked through left-wing propaganda espoused by liberation theologians and academia. They were fearful they would end up with mass demonstrations to help gut the military through a sizeable faith-based opposition to the government and the SADF.

The South Africa military was all that was standing between civilization and a communist takeover. The conflict in South Africa was more deadly and sinister than any exchange of fire in any contact, whether in Angola, Mozambique or north of the Limpopo. It was a total war for the hearts and minds and the very soul of a nation. Before they could instil a humanist socialist government, they had first to control the faith-based churches, negating traditional theology. Their goal was to replace God with their man-made god, a god whose laws would include the right to murder.

One of my line functions, being able to move comfortably in the Christian environment, was to have contacts with church mission groups, NGOs and anyone doing relief work to the north of South Africa that could be useful. In a counter-terrorist role, having people on the ground is the very kernel, the living heart and soul of intelligence. The shooting or removal of enemies only comes once you have established who, what, when and how to kill. Killing is easy; finding the right ones to kill has always been the hard part of the equation. If you want to know if they have a big dog in the yard before climbing over the fence, ask the local postman; it's as simple as that. You have to communicate and learn about your target or target groups, and the only way you can do this is by getting close to them, or by personally getting close through the opposition you have created. My role now would, in all probability, lead to the death of more hostiles than all my shooting and claymore mines ever did. To be effective, someone somewhere labours over maps and photos, working on target acquisition. I always wondered why Military Intelligence and Special Branch got so excited when the special forces came back with a positive response.

My portfolio at times seemed extensive, and in 1987 I was briefed for another external operation. I would this time piggyback on the back of a Christian NGO and make an entry into Mozambique via Botswana through Zambia. It was a circuitous route when the shortest way would have been through Zimbabwe. How the Botswana–Zambia route came about I have no idea or recollection. My brief was to work through another Australian contact named Gee (FRELIMO later imprisoned this fellow Australian; I am not sure who he was as everyone used different names) who had good communications with the rebel group RENAMO (Mozambique National Resistance), who had been initially trained and supplied by the Rhodesian SAS. RENAMO was an asset at that time as they were keeping FRELIMO busy and slowing down the southward terrorist movement and generally destabilizing that country. To give some idea of the web and world I worked in, I was once on my way to a particular company in another African country and I bumped into Bob Mac (later KIA in Sierra Leone), a one-time officer in the SAS, an American who had supposedly gone back to the US. There he was exiting the aeroplane I was now boarding, having visited the same company outside of South Africa – smoke and mirrors are like that. I was to open a land route to RENAMO bases by which South Africa could supply and train the rebels. The small team consisted of one intelligence operator, namely me, along with three unaware workers from an NGO, two British and one South African, all good people with no nefarious plans at all.

We travelled through Botswana without any problems and entered Zambia via the Kazungula ferry, now operational again having been sunk by the Rhodesian SAS some years before. It was strange to be on the ferry; I knew the divers who sent it to the bottom. I had a bit of a personal laugh about that. The laughter came to an abrupt halt some miles down the road after we had cleared customs on the Zambian side. We were stopped and arrested at the very first military roadblock we came across. Had they been expecting us? It appeared so. I can't say this was the happiest day of my life, although for the Zambians it wasn't looking too bad as they drove us back to Kazungula police station at gunpoint. The first slight was to be entirely stripped, searched and made to stand in front of a funny little man sitting behind a battered desk, with scruffy bits of paper and an old book placed on top of it, signs of his officialdom and the great leap forward for another independent African nation. He did ask some questions, but most of the time he wrote in the scruffy book.

I had completed escape and evasion courses in the army. The Australians call them the conduct of a prisoner of war. They later scrapped these courses when someone came up with an excellent idea: the money would better used training troops on how not to get caught. I had also done various dark phases on selection, but this was a little different as my captors were now real, and they did not like me at all.

To start with, they were raw and of limited intelligence – stupid is more apt – and they had no one in control. They could kill me and say I'd try to run, or shoot me and then bury me in a shallow grave. The one thing I did learn from all the armies I'd served in was when in doubt say nothing other than number, rank and name. This revelation would have been a deal-breaker at that time: sharing my past seemed a poor option. Saying nothing was the best course of action. I was not going to be silly enough to admit I was in the army, and as it was, I never had to. After some time, he asked where and how I got the scars on my body.

'I fell off a motorbike.'

He did not believe me but it went in the book. Told to get dressed, I had a strange feeling about this: no one had kicked me in the head, no rifle butts. When would that start and why hadn't it yet started? They were unsure of who we were. Then it began: the bag over the head and the chains. The first cell, totally bare except the cement floor, was the filthiest and most disgusting place I had ever experienced, with old blood and all kinds of excrement and who knows what all over the walls. One does not have to be a rocket scientist to know you're in trouble when dumped in a place like that.

First, herded all together then one by one each was removed and taken. Where? To be shot or tortured? in a situation like that you never know. Being left alone in the dingy cell, I heard no gunshots so assumed they had just separated us for security reasons. Then I listened: some way off or was it next door, their singing came through the walls. They were all alive, singing 'Waltzing Matilda', out of tune, I might add. At least they still had all their teeth, which was encouraging.

The pushing and pulling and being dumped in the back of a vehicle with hoods and chains came the next morning. I was trying to think but I was not entirely sure about what, as I had not slept very well. I missed my bed. We drove some way and then I smelled avgas; we were at an airstrip. The first thing that went through my mind as they bundled us into the aeroplane was they were going to dump us once airborne. The engines started up. I heard a voice in perfect English, with an African accent, telling our guards to shoot us if we did anything untoward. These are not sound instructions to give to an AK-wielding semi-literate inside an aeroplane as it's taxiing to get off the ground. As I said, stupid is the more descriptive word. Stupid is as stupid does.

The plane landed with a full cargo: no one had been thrown out. More pushing and pulling, on and off trucks, knocks, bangs, unpleasantness, then they pulled the hoods off. In front of me were two massive doors. I was inside a dimly light tunnel. To my rear another two identical double doors that I had unknowingly just come through. I had entered another world and a very uncertain future if I had any at all. This was the real thing. No one knew we had even been stopped and apprehended. The only upside was it was cool. My throat was parched; I'd had no water for some time. Now we were led to a small door in the tunnel, walls to the right; we were ushered into a dingy reception room. African diplomacy was at work. Our station and position afforded us the treatment that any white suspect in black Africa could expect. We were from South Africa and therefore dangerous.

After processing, we stood in front of those formidable double doors waiting for them to open. None of us knew once the gates opened and shut behind us just how long this new life as prisoners would last. The doors swung open: the scene that faced me was like something out of Beau Geste, bright African sun bounced and reflected off a white, sunbaked, barren quadrangle. To my front, through the glare, I could see a massive prison yard stretching out its welcome. After being in the dark yet cool interior of the interrogation room, the light stung my eyes and the heat washed over me. Lined up one behind the other in chains, we shuffled out of the shade into the harsh glare of the prison yard, with hundreds of dark brown bloodshot eyes watching. Mother would not have felt comfortable. Guards escorted us to our cell.

No blankets, no bedding: it wasn't needed as the heat was unbearable; it would get even more so once the fifteen-by-fifteen-foot cell was full. For the next three days we would be taken, one at a time, from our cell, hooded, barefoot and in chains, then transported across town to headquarters. Whose? Who would be our interrogators today: the army, military police or some other intelligence organ? The remaining three were left back at the prison, wondering. Questions pleasantly asked. Then one would say something in Afrikaans. I had no idea what he was saying: I was English-speaking, then being knocked off the chair and the hood roughly placed over my head again. Then dragged outside, I could feel the sun on me, but no sound. Where was I?

'You think we can't kill you because you're white? I'll show you.'

Things were not going well. Then I heard the weapon being drawn and cocked. I knew what it was like to be shot. I recall the pistol, hot metal rammed in the back of my neck. I held my breath. I wondered why I did.

Click.

Then shouting in an Africa language I did not understand. For my benefit, a lot of verbal abuse and suggestions.

'Don't shoot him in the head. Shoot him up his asshole.' Pistol forced between the cheeks of my buttocks.

Click.

I was shaking I think, I don't remember. Dragged back inside, hood off, pleasant new voice speaking to me, turns and yells at people in the room who scurry away and bring me water.

Pleasant voice: 'Are you all right, major?'

I don't respond, I am not a major. Friendly voice puts a hand on my shoulder and pats me gently.

I say, 'Thank you for the water.'

'You're all right now. These people are uncivilized.'

I wanted to scream or cry but didn't. The treatment would go on for the next three days, played out with various different scenarios. Never once did I think they wouldn't shoot; every click just meant they had made up a new way to kill me. I did not inform the other three of my treatment. I was older, had wounds over my body and they thought I was the leader. Major? I was not. I was just hitching a ride. It was a battle of wills. The first seventy-two hours were the worst. The Zambians knew they had netted something, but they did not know what.

In the small cell that held sixteen-plus bodies with no beds was a prisoner named Sipho. An operator from a reconnaissance unit, Sipho had been detained in Zambia and handed over to the ANC, who tortured him for a protracted period, before being handed back to the Zambians, and whose cell I now shared. Such was the trauma of his ordeal, one had to listen to him cry in his sleep every night. Sipho had been a member of the Rhodesian African Rifles before he moved to South Africa at the end of the Rhodesian war. He joined the SADF and operated in a reconnaissance role. In 1980, recruited into Military Intelligence, he became a covert operator until 1985 when the Zambian police detained him and handed him over to the ANC for interrogation. My being in the same cell could have serious consequences. There was always the danger we'd met or crossed paths at some time. I had also got three innocent young people involved.

To put the whole thing into some perspective, in 1988 while operating in Zimbabwe, three operatives were detained, tried and given the death sentence; they spent some years appealing the sentence when on Death Row. Their sentences were eventually commuted to life. They served eighteen years before being freed in 2006 and sent back to South Africa. In any other war, they would have been POWs. Alternatively, the government would have negotiated their release at the end of hostilities. South Africa had dozens of men and some female operatives sentenced to lengthy prison terms and most were left to rot.

I don't think the three with me realized the seriousness of the situation. We were foreign nationals; we may have been from an NGO but to the Zambians we were South African agents. The South African government had this appalling track record of dropping most of their agents like a dead dog, apart from one or two high-profile captures who had Afrikaans names. We were acceptable losses.

My detention order was dated Thursday, 8 October 1987. On the morning of Wednesday, 14 October 1987, the interrogations stopped. I hoped they would not start again. Unbeknown to me, the Commonwealth Heads of Government conference had started on Tuesday, 13 October 1987 and would end on Saturday, 17 October. My revocation of detention was signed on 21 October, the next Wednesday.

South Africa had been a country in turmoil since the Soweto Uprising of 1976 with riots, civil unrest and violence. The South African Police were able to deal with public disorder due to its high degree of training and its vast intelligence network. At no time was there any likelihood of the ANC taking power. However, both the local and overseas media had a political agenda. They played up the unrest. It did not go unnoticed by the loosely knit group of gangsters called Commonwealth Heads of Government. The vast majority of them were leaders from countries that had held one-man-one-vote-once-type elections. As they gathered at Nassau in the Bahamas in 1985, the clarion call was for South Africa to dismantle apartheid. South Africa refused to comply.

In 1985 a hotchpotch of so-called influential people titled the Eminent Persons Group (EPG) was cobbled together, comprising has-been presidents, leaders of starving third-world states and liberation theologians. With stars in their eyes and boundless enthusiasm, all laboured under the misconstrued idea that they would solve South Africa's problems and get a Nobel Peace Prize and of course the cash benefits that went along with it. Unfortunately, or fortunately, depending on where you were standing at the time, things did not go well for this particular EPG mission. The SADF then launched a series of successful special forces strikes against ANC targets in Zimbabwe and Botswana, simultaneously with airstrikes against Zambia by the South African Air Force. The EPG got into a hissy fit, sulked and went home in May 1986.

In 1987, the Commonwealth Heads of Government Conference was held in Canada. One of the main items on the agenda was South Africa. Britain's Margaret Thatcher and US President Ronald Reagan tried to inject some sanity into the conference, using such words as 'peaceful dialogue'. For all Black Africa's bellicosity, they were all heavily dependent on South Africa and western funding to keep themselves in a lifestyle they were not deserving of. Thatcher put great emphasis on the aid Great Britain was funnelling into Africa, and hoped that they would all resolve the apartheid issue through dialogue and diplomatic means. The conference, however, spent most the time trying to get harsher sanctions imposed on South Africa, an act that both Reagan and Thatcher vehemently opposed although outnumbered.

What is said and done in public is for public consumption. It is not reality. Achievements at these conferences – the majority of the agreements made – were done behind closed doors. Publicly the most rabid and vociferous opponent to anything Reagan or Thatcher had proposed was the corrupt, screeching megalomaniac Kenneth Kaunda, the president of Zambia. Kaunda's attack was promptly blunted when Thatcher put in her counterattack asking why he, Kaunda, had detained three young British subjects, who at that very time where being subjected to torture and inhumane conditions? Thatcher was able to gain the moral high ground and a short time after the conclusion of this conference all four of us, under escort by the Zambian Special Branch, were rushed to the border and sent packing back to South Africa.

Once back, it was agreed I would no longer be going north again as I had made a name for myself and, had I gone, there was a degree of certainty I would not get out a second time.

My job internally would become more intense. I discovered that the SADF did not need the line of communication I opened with RENAMO. They had recently dropped tons of equipment in a massive airdrop over a period of almost two weeks, and an old friend who had soldiered with me in Rhodesia, a decorated colonel in the South African Special Forces, had supposedly opened the corridor to RENAMO. He told me there was no need for my efforts. It was a set-up, more than likely to ease Thatcher's progress at the Vancouver conference. Had we been set up by the British or the South Africans, or was it just lousy joss that we of all people got taken into custody over the dates of the conference? The world of smoke and mirrors is a strange world, and most times very dangerous. I henceforth would view all operations with a jaundiced eye and always submitted one plan but had a Plan B and changed my operational procedures once on the ground. I did not trust my masters, but I would still take their money because that's what I do.

In the early 1990s, the now-unbanned ANC had executive members flitting all around the globe. I retrieved a five-shot .38 revolver, five rounds loaded ready to use from a dead letter drop. After the shoot, I was to drop the gun and keep on walking. Someone else would pick up the firearm. My target would come out of the airport and have to walk across an open carpark. My mark approached from my right, wore a red scarf and had kind of a bouncy walk. He looked very pleased with himself: had he come through the airport six months ago the security police would have lifted him. Things were different now. I was about to do it when I got *stop stop stop*. I kept on my line of approach but slowed down. We passed very close: seconds ago, a dead man walking, now he would carry on and become part of what they had planned, but he would die of cancer before he became too bothersome.

In 1990 President F.W. de Klerk dropped the bombshell: the ANC was to be unbanned and Mandela released from prison. I knew the wheels were about to come off. I started to train various groups to work in an operational role. My intelligence work was learning to make war, much the same as in Laos. The government could not be trusted, and although the military was committed to the fight, I could see signs that the National Party would at some time capitulate. I was getting a lot of intelligence coming in. I knew what the ANC was doing and thinking long before it got to their members on the ground.

I considered getting my wife out of the country and to a safe place – back home in Australia. This unravelling motivated me to get Barbara out. I would come back and take control of my teams once she was safe. Before I left, there would be many angry meetings between the military and CSI.

I was tasked through 1993 to travel to Natal to start training KwaZulu operatives. In the first quarter of 1994, a security company or Zulu self-protection unit was formed with the consent of King Goodwill Zwelithini and Zulu Prime Minister Mangosuthu Buthelezi. It became too high profile. The commander was an inexperienced university student who to the best of my knowledge had no or minimal operational experience in the military. My due diligence showed that he was put through university by South African Special Branch that picked up the tab for services rendered. I had no problem with this at all, good luck to the guy. I did meet him a few times when I had students working for me. I am not saying he was not academically bright; I just thought he was an arrogant prick. And later, on competent authority, I found out he was a double working for MI6.

The military was still tasking me to run agents inside various left-wing political groups such as the United Democratic Front and the ANC. The End Conscription Campaign had become irrelevant now that the shooting between the ANC and the Zulu IFP (Inkatha Freedom Party) was about to start. I was using their funds to set up the training of civilian groups for when the wheels fell off, as I knew they would. It was not too long after this that the order came down not to engage the ANC whom I thought was the enemy. Strangely enough, my job became more intense. All the indications pointed to South Africa sliding into civil war. It was so close I could smell it.

On 20 March 1994, I was in the centre of Johannesburg when the Zulus, the IFP, marched on the ANC HQ. Things were reasonably orderly. Then within seconds, I came under heavy fire. I don't think it was a personal thing, like, 'Oh look! There's Rob Brown. Let's get him.' Bearing down on the ANC was an impi of 50,000 unhappy Zulus with traditional as well as automatic weapons. Shell House, the ANC headquarters, was about to become another 1789 Bastille and maybe every bit as defining for them as that day was for the French. They were not about to let that happen. There was gunfire, selective and semi-automatic, with bullets flying all over the place.

Thirty-one marchers were killed and 276 wounded; how many would later die of their wounds remains unknown: there were no official figures. It was one hell of a bloody contact.

It took two years for me to close down one of my principal covert operations called Veterans for Victory. I still ran agents and would not close it down until all the loyal people were secured financially, along with their safety assured, which meant destruction of documents. It was one of the saddest jobs I had had to do; many were young men and women who just wanted to fight to save their country. Military Intelligence held signed cheques relating to my activities in case something was to happen to me; for the same reason, they had keys to the office. I cleared the accounts before they could and paid my people.

*   *   *

Barbara and I arrived in Australia in 1995. I am an Australian, so being in Australia was no hardship for me. Australia is clean and efficient and expensive. Everything works as it should. It is a beautiful country to relax in and wait until you die. By the time Barbara got to Australia, she was emotionally exhausted. She was every bit a casualty of war as any wounded soldier and over-fought trooper. She was like most Rhodesians when they had to flee to South Africa. When we arrived in Australia, we were much like refugees, or Barbara was. I was just a penniless Australian returning from a world tour that had lasted for many years. I can't say my family had ever been bubbling with enthusiasm or interest whenever I returned home. I don't think they understood me or what I did. In my line of work, it is tough to quantify or give a detailed job description. Needless to say, when I returned this time with a wife who painted her nails red and did her hair every day, they had a problem understanding her as well: why would they not? I was family and they never really appreciated me. You could cut the atmosphere with a knife. I did not know what I had done; surely, it could not be because Barbara was South African?

Some short time later, some clarity to their mindset in regards to our stay was displayed. The SAS often operates in a covert role when on external or cross-border tasks, as do most special forces units. We work, fight or do our job or whatever other euphemism one uses, in places not known by the general public. About these things, the ordinary world is meant not to know. It is called acceptable deniability. Governments don't want large parts of their population to know or understand the machinations that they take part in for their political ends. Sometimes if secret operations are successful then for political expediency or gain, the military will make the general public aware of what they have done, but this usually is a political call.

I don't know how it came about. I think I mentioned something about the wet weather affecting my wounds. Keith's son, who knew little or nothing about me or special forces, chirped up and started relating how I had had the 'accident'. Where he got this information, I have no idea. The military would have informed my family that I was in hospital doing well or not so well after an incident. No way would anyone give them any in-depth knowledge of areas, locations or contact details; it is not good security. After this brief one-sided exchange, Keith jumped up like a scalded cat, saying, 'That's enough, that's enough! We don't want any of that here!' (Now where had I heard that before?) They had watched too many American movies. What did they think I was going to do? Go to pieces and kill them with a plastic fork whilst they slept?

The atmosphere that had been continuously present since our arrival was now made more than clear. It was apparent they had reservations and some apprehensions. Having a professional soldier in their home had made them wary. Were they waiting for some catalyst to send me over that imaginary line? In their mind, all soldiers inevitably must from time to time go over the edge with violent and uncontrolled acts, as portrayed in the movies. And of course, this psychotic, unbalanced war veteran was accompanied by a beautiful woman, who was from the wicked, evil apartheid South Africa. We were just too much for them psychologically. My family comprises ordinary Australians, average people who have a limited understanding of things outside their comfort zone. And why would they not, as most of their information comes from sound bites on TV?

Then one day, my mother turned on me and asked, 'Is your wife Jewish?', vocalized with such venom it was like someone had punched me. What do you say to something like that? Her grandmother came from Odessa, Ukraine, and her name was Shari Gosse. The final straw was the day I came back from a run. I could not find Barbara. I eventually discovered her sitting on a park bench, alone. It was the first time I had ever seen Barbara cry. She wanted to go home, so that's what I did: I took her home to South Africa. Petty, ignorant people hunted Barbara like a wounded doe. Like Elizabeth, she never stood a chance against such unbridled animosity; nothing had changed.

On my return to Africa, I went to South Sudan. I spent five months up there. While I was up north, Barbara started another business and a very successful one at that. Her business grew, so I never had to go back to work in South Africa. I suppose one would have called me a kept man. I was still running and training, although I did not work in my profession again for some time.

Barbara and I travelled a lot overseas. There were times when Barbara would fly high as she did when we first met, and there were times when she would spend days in bed just sleeping. She went to doctors, took pills, and at times it even looked as if she was once more on top of the world. I had little or no knowledge of psychological illness and therefore had no way of knowing what Barbara's problem was or how bad it was. I was an ignorant onlooker. I understood gunshot wounds, torn bodies, landmines and mortars and, of course, an attitude of indifference to the hardship. I had no idea about mental scars at all. Barbara had seen a psychiatrist who gave her pills, plenty of them. Then one day she came to me and made the simple statement: 'I can handle this. I don't need pills. Plus they make me feel ill.' But she couldn't handle it, could she?

On 27 April 2004, eight years after we had returned from Australia, my wife Barbara blew her brains out, using my .38 snub-nose revolver that she had taken from beneath my pillow only seconds before. Time of death: 0800 plus or minus. I knew she was dead; with a head wound like that she had to be. I have watched men, different kinds of men at various times in various places, get killed by various means; none of them had wanted to die or had been looking for death. Barbara, on the other hand, had wanted to. All she had to do was walk around the bed, put her hand under the pillow, retrieve the weapon, point it and squeeze the trigger. All deliberate acts.

I might sound matter of fact, almost callous, indifferent. But at the time I was in a total state of shock. In a contact when troops are killed, the others around them are busy doing things like staying alive, finding a target or winning the firefight amid a great deal of noise, movement and shouting. Whatever the outcome, someone removes the bodies, someone takes control and you regroup, call in casevac and then move on. Operational soldiers after a time learn what to do with bodies. Looking down at Barbara's body, I did not have a clue what to do. I had learned no procedures on how to deal with the body of a dead wife. I had IAs (Immediate Action drills) for almost everything military, but not for a wife.

I stopped thinking. I was not busy. I had nothing to do. There was nothing to fight back with. No words of encouragement. Not that Barbara would have heard as half her head was missing. I was not busy on a radio or yelling orders or receiving orders. There was no 'I'm coming through' – no movement or excitement, not even fear to motivate to overcome the inertia. In front of me was not some cobber or trooper on the ground: it was my wife, the woman I had loved. Panic took over. I found the stairs but don't remember going down into the office. I saw the phone but forgot the numbers I needed. I don't know much of what I did or did not say. All I knew I was calling, but no one was coming. I remember thinking, 'Parks, get Parks. He's regiment. Parks will help,' so I phoned Doug. It was like being in contact. You yell down the radio, 'Contact! Contact!' At that time, you don't want a conversation – what you want to hear is 'Roger' then instinctively you know something is happening somewhere. You don't know if they are going to give you top cover or what. You have no idea just what they are going to do. You do know when the voice comes back with 'Roger' or 'Stand by' it means something is happening – someone back there where you can't see is working for you.

The police and the medics did arrive. Did I phone them? Don't know, can't remember. Did I call the ambulance? Don't know, can't remember. I do recall the police were two of the fattest black cops I had ever seen. They were more interested in what was in the house than the body upstairs. Then a white couple, a man and woman detective team, arrived who specialized in domestic violence and suicide.

At last, I had professional people who looked as if they knew what to do. Could I have stopped her? Maybe, had we been closer. Would she have lived? Possibly, but for a short time, as the head wound was terrible. If you're a professional soldier, death is a reality, an ever-present shadow lurking and waiting. One never gets used to it; you learn to live with it. However, this death was personal, painful and close. It hurt. It was the worst death I had ever seen. I have never asked why! Not then or ever – no never, no, not once.

I was answering the detectives' questions. I think I was making sense, and then Doug arrived. He came through the door that had been left open by the medics as they went out. He just pushed past the fat cops and asked them what they were doing, so they slunk away. Then Sergeant Parker of B Squadron Special Air Service, a man who has no time for people but loves dogs, who has the world's worst attitude with anyone who is not regiment, put his arms around me and just held me. Thirty-six years of conflict, killing and death and I had kept it all together. I lost it and cried like that two-year-old who had dropped his bottle.

There can be many reasons a beautiful woman with a passion for life ends up killing herself. As hard as one tries, you will never get a definitive answer. I stood alone in that large, empty house. I would clean the blood-spattered bedroom walls sometime later. She had so much going for her.

Chapter 7

Unscheduled Death and Iraq

One hour of life crowded to the full with glorious action
And filled with noble risks
Is worth whole years of those mean observances
Of paltry decorum in which men steal through existence,
Like sluggish water through a marsh without honour
or observation

Walter Scott

After some considerable time, the police came and did forensic tests on my hands. The two special detectives and the fat cops had left. Strangely enough, medics do not take the bodies away, as I thought. The ambulance service takes victims that are alive to change them into patients; coroners remove bodies. After everyone had left, I was once more alone with Barbara's body. Then the coroner's van came; they put her in a body bag and bumped her down the stairs; there is not much dignity in death. Doug did stay with me for a long time, but then he had to go home. So, there I was in this vast, rambling house, alone; the silence was deafening. If ever there was a time for reflection, most certainly this was it.

I understand grief, but I had no idea that when someone dies, other than a soldier, the people close to them have an awful lot to do. Someone has to identify the body. I got Doug to go and do that; it was not a job I wanted. Then you have to find a coffin. Do you know you can spend as much on a box as you can on a luxury motor vehicle? Death is a growth industry; the more people there are in the world, the more people are going to die because everybody dies. So, if you're in the coffin business and death, you just have got to make money.

A pastor at a church used to say funerals are for the living; it gives them closure; I suppose it also eases their conscience. The dead know nothing about the size or quality of the coffin. I also had no idea that there were so many euphemisms for the word 'dead'. Doug came with me to look at some coffins; it was not the most pleasant shopping trip that either of us has ever done. We usually hung around gun shops and places that sold good stuff for our profession. They were not going to cremate Barbara in a blanket, were they? So, it was coffin-buying time. It was just another unpleasant job, resulting from the whole beastly business that had enveloped me in the past days. I think the reality of death was starting to get to Doug by that time, but I also knew that my situation was made more manageable by having him around. I am not the meanest person in the world, I did love my wife and I was devastated by her death. However, I could see no point in being involved in a charade of coffins with brass handrails and cucumber sandwiches on white bread with no crusts, which most people would not eat and would end up being taken home by the catering staff. Only seven people were at the chapel. Six were from the church; they had not known Barbara well at all, but it was kind of them to come. Only one person attending the funeral could be called a close friend of Barbara's, a man called A.K., and he was a Muslim so would not be eating any of the sandwiches. Without sounding ghoulish, I wondered whether they cremated the coffin along with the body or did they recycle?

I started to slowly settle down. One of the worst days was when a friend called Vic asked me where my wife was. I could not speak. I had to walk away. From then on, there would be lots of firsts. I rarely left the bedroom, let alone the house. Doug and his wife Teresa were there for me. I also had Vic and his wife whose first husband had hanged himself. She had found him. The thing about Barbara's death was that it was so in your face. It was traumatic in its closeness, violent in its application and ugly in its final result. I slept in the same room with the bloody walls. The chairs covered in Barbara's blood would have to go. I put it all off until Doug told me, 'If you don't clean up, it's going to start to smell a bit.' When the troops are stressed, give them something to do. So that's what I did. I stood alone in that quiet, empty bedroom and then tore up the carpets and scrubbed the walls.

Everything had belonged to Barbara – the house, the car, everything was in her name. When I took stock, apart from my clothes and my firearms, I had a great big fat nothing. Had I informed the bank that Barbara was dead, they would have closed the account. Then I would not even have had money for food: I had no credit cards, no job and no bank account. I had been too idle to live my own life. I was a passenger on Barbara's Good Ship Lollipop that she had just scuttled. Someone once told me, that after a traumatic event, you don't do anything or make any important decisions for at least twelve months. Under normal circumstances, good advice, but if I was going to wait that long I would starve. Banks are robbers of widows and orphans, and the vulnerable. I was now one of the vulnerable. The vultures were circling. The less I told the bank, the less they would know and the higher the chance of my survival. I went and asked Barbara's clients to make payments into another account where I had signing powers. The bank, of course, realized Barbara was dead: the mortgage had lapsed and no money had come into the account. They very graciously told me I had six weeks to sell the house and get out.

I don't know if the bank forgot about me or what. I had no way of paying the mortgage, but after that first notification to get out so that they could sell the house, I never heard from them again for over a year. In the meantime, I took a job outside the country. When I came back to South Africa, I was able to sell the house within weeks, and I paid the bank back all it was owed. My new world without Barbara looked uncertain at best. I was a man in his late fifties, with no job, and in an African country that was sliding into recession. The lights would start to go out sometime soon. My problem was I had run out of time. I was 57 years old with no war in the offing. I had been tagging along with Barbara just for the ride. I had become so dependent on her. The phone rang off the hook every day: people wanted money and a lot of it. At the last count, Barbara had over thirteen credit cards, all maxed out, and that was not including unique client cards for five-star hotels in the UK and the US, executive flying clubs and personal loans that I knew nothing about. I jumped every time the phone rang. With regards to Mrs Brown's outstanding accounts – 'Can you, please have Barbara phone us?' – Barbara had been a very, very naughty girl. Fortunately, I had an antenuptial agreement, but it did not stop the phone calls. Many came after hours, and I also had the inevitable personal visits. I had collected money, but only enough for necessary costs and they weren't getting any of that. Then even that ran out. I started to look around for some way of making a living to buy tinned fish for what must have been the most spoilt and well-travelled cat in the world. He would sit there looking at me with a knowing look that conveyed the message, 'Boy, are you in trouble and when is the missus coming back.' However, she wasn't coming back, was she? My situation was difficult, and it was not going to improve any time soon. I had not informed the cat. I did not want to worry him.

I heard companies were looking for people. I started to get back into the loop about a job in Iraq. I pulled out my CV and dusted it off. My last job was in South Sudan in 1996 and that was eight years ago. I sent my CV to security companies all over the world, and waited and waited. Eventually, I got to talk to a recruiting woman called Mickey, and built up a relationship with her – or maybe I was just lonely. Late one night as I was travelling across town, I got a call from her.

'How long will it take you to move to go to Iraq?'

'About two weeks.'

'Not good enough. We need you on the plane by Thursday.'

That was only four days away. I'd have to get the cat into a cattery and someone to house-sit; lots of things needed doing. Would I have time? I would make it work, somehow. I agreed I would collect my ticket on Thursday at the airport and fly out that day. I found a house-sitter and the cat stayed home.

Barbara killed herself on 22 April 2004. I flew out of South Africa on 22 July 2004, destination Iraq.

* * *

Being a professional soldier over the years, I have seen many changes with each war. Every new conflict has its own sayings and lexicon, Iraq would be no different. We now had F-16s on station, meaning somewhere high up in the heavens out of sight was silent death waiting to be called down. We used a GPS not a compass and a bit of string, and IEDs replaced vehicle landmines.

Landing in Kuwait, I was picked up and driven to the company villa where I would spend two days waiting for a place on a US military flight. A well-run and professional company had hired me, unlike many companies working in Iraq. Golf Company had all my documentation sorted and emailed to me along with their SOPs – standard operational procedures – and even my position on the gun cars, what my line function was, and, most important, insurance and pay scale. With modern technology working from London to Kuwait and across to South Africa and back through the chain, the contract was expedited within hours once they had my full CV.

Golf was a British company, under direct US military command, registered in Hong Kong, but run by the Brits. I had no idea who my immediate boss was, much like when in Laos. What I did know was the project officer was an American, I believe a civilian who may have been USMC. His 2IC was also an American and a civilian, probably ex-military as well. I found both of them to be gentlemen, who had a lot to contend with as many of the young men in the company were what I called 'Gucci soldiers'. When I first got there, I introduced myself to a gentleman who had a distinctly plummy accent, much like my colonel in the British Para Regiment back in 1969. A Rupert of Ruperts, he came across as a good person. He disappeared a day or so later and I never came across him again.

I sat on my bed in the Kuwaiti villa. People were rotating out as I was going in. One of those leaving was a medic. I always found the trauma medics from the US were first class. Americans take their life support very seriously. Talking to him, I found out a convoy had been hit a day or so before and from his description, it was not good. I was filling a dead man's shoes or taking his place on a vehicle. Stories are always more dramatic in the telling, but I sat on that bed and thought to myself, 'Robert, have you done the right thing?' But there was no going back, the same as in Laos where they owned all the transport. I had a good talk with myself then put my head down and had one of the best night's sleep since Barbara had topped herself. Tomorrow I would present myself to Air Movements, and the US Air Force would fly me back to war. The same as they had done in October 1968, because it's what I do.

I was transported by an air-condition upmarket vehicle to the hangar on a military base in Kuwait. I believe it was a Kuwaiti Air Force base. I mention this as there were many security companies and service delivery contractors working in Iraqi, often with inadequate logistics, which led to injury and even death of some of their contractors. I know of one case where personnel flew to Kuwait and were then left to enter Iraqi any way they could. One team ferried across the border, hiding under a tarpaulin in the back of a vehicle. Another group was halfway through a checkpoint with no documentation. Someone opened fire and a member of the team got shot. Today he lives with a colostomy. I have no problem with contractors doing this: it was very much the same as what I'd done when I first contracted into Laos.

I was fortunate to be contracted to a highly professional security company. It was the only operational civilian company in Iraq to mount and use what are called crew-fed weapons, any weapon system that requires a crew of more than one to operate it, such as heavy machine guns and rocket launchers. In our case, we had the American Mk 19 grenade launcher, which was a 40mm belt-fed automatic launcher, and the .50 Browning machine gun. Our weapons were on hire from the US military. How did a private company get access to these? Don't ask: I genuinely don't know.

On arrival at the airbase, my name was already on the airlift manifest. The only requirements were that I had to have my helmet and Kevlar which we were all told to sit on, suggesting that flights in had taken some small-arms ground fire in the past. We landed at a military airbase just outside of Mosul. The name Mosul is the anglicized name for Al-Mawṣil, which is how it was spelled on my 1:10,000 map. One of the call signs collected me from the airstrip and it was directly off the flight and off to war. I got my kit off the plane and away we went in a soft-skinned Toyota, no armour. An AK47 was passed to me. No briefing except: 'If they shoot, shoot back and don't let any civilian vehicles get close.' I lost count of the number of times our .50 Browning opened fire on civilian vehicles. I got tired of calling to our Gurkha gunner if we were under fire. He was just brushing off any cars that he thought looked dangerous or came too close. In the end, I just let him get on with it and use his own judgement. Vehicles that get closer than twenty or thirty metres are a danger. When they detonate from that distance, you're going to get some of the blast and shrapnel. Some of our people would die. So, brush them off or light them up, and sort it out later. Not being military, we did not fall under military law. Not being Iraqi we did not fall under civilian rule either. We were a law unto ourselves. Many times the vehicle carrying the explosive device would have on board a family – women and kids – so they could get close. Islamic terrorism has no concern for life – all they want to do is kill the *kafir*, the infidel. The man operating the gun would have to make a decision when to open fire.

In the first six weeks in Iraq working out of Mosul on convoy duty, I was IED'd three times. I sat and worked it out that with that many IEDs in so short a space of time, the percentages of getting killed were high. Frankly, it did not worry me over much at all. It's not that I am brave. I have in the past been so terrified that all I wanted to do was throw away my rifle and run away. Fear has a distinct smell and taste; it's almost tangible. I could smell this unease when around others but I was no longer affected by it. I no longer cared. There was nothing for me back in South Africa or any place any more. Other than the cat, everything had gone with Barbara. Like Celeste, she had taught me to enjoy the finer things in life, admittedly at other people's expense. I had now gone back to drinking water out of a mug or an army canteen; no more fine crystal for Robert: refinement no longer existed in my world. The big plus was I firmly believed that this was where I was supposed to be at that time. I felt comfortable with it. Golf Global was a high-breed security company. I was a high-breed special forces soldier, somewhat battered and traumatized but never the less still whole and functioning.

The company members were a mixture of individuals. Some were seasoned soldiers – Special Forces, Royal Marines, US Marines, SAS and even an Irish Foreign Legionnaire. A lot, however, had no military pedigree and were chancers or from territorial units of the British Army, maybe one or two from 21 SAS, and from their age and demeanour, they would have done very little before Iraq. One or two had just done a civilian security course or read a book. Some were simply on an ego trip – they were not professional soldiers, but 'Gucci soldiers' who had all the gear and little else. There were, however, some good ones. My platoon commander was a lot younger than me but one of the better ones, a Royal Marine. A lot of people did not like him, but he knew his stuff. I thought he was a good leader. Then there was another Royal Marine who had fought in the Falklands, a mature, quiet man but good at what he did. The American medics were among the best I had seen – all very competent.

Many of the younger members did not like me. On more than one occasion, they told me it was time to hang up my parachute boots. I was there with another old special forces soldier whom I had soldiered with in Rhodesia. Paul was a knowledgeable and skilled special forces operator who had seen a lot of action in the Rhodesian war. He was a bit pedantic for some and from time to time would tell me I was cuffing it. Maybe I was, but I was tired. Paul was the same age as me, and often said they didn't like older people: we showed them up. The laughable thing was one call sign used to call their section commander 'the old man'. I suppose age is a subjective thing as both Paul and I, and the Royal Marine who had been in the Falklands War, could have been his father, or even his grandfather.

It was at times dog eat dog. Due to the high salaries we were being paid, there was always someone trying to squeeze someone else out, so he could get his mate brought in. If it had not been for the single-mindedness of Tommo, my platoon commander, I would have been out of work after my first R&R. That Royal Marine saved my job many times. Not because I was a lousy operator, but so many people wanted to get their chum in on the pay scale, and they'd stab anyone in the back to make it happen. Plus, as Paul had said, they didn't like older people. There was little loyalty or esprit de corps. On more than one occasion someone would leave on R&R and be told once out of Iraq not to come back. But for all the problem children there were some very professional people, interesting characters who had been in the business for a time. Good people.

One person, who no way in the world looked like a soldier, had been a real honest-to-god spy in the Cold War, and who had worked as a high-speed signaller behind the Iron Curtain; a little roly-poly man with a red face and mild manner, he was an exceedingly pleasant man. He was another one who did not fit, not macho enough for some of the younger troops. There was also a British bobby, definitely SAS before or after his police thing. His sister was in some church or other. When I spoke with him, he was having problems coming to terms with the fact a close friend from the regiment had recently been killed. I was now filling that space. It was not a personal thing between us, more of a spiritual thing. He was one of the more balanced people even if somewhat conflicted.

We had a rapid turnover of operators. Some went on R&R and never got a ticket back, or they were squeezed out because of personality problems. Some I remember well. Others came and went in a short space of time. It was not for everyone. I had a military policeman come on to my car. I don't know how he got to Iraq. He did one operation then asked to leave; he was only there for about seventy-two hours. He complained for the full fourteen hours of the operation. Some I remember because they were pigs, others because they were good at the job. On more than one occasion I would have to speak with some of them and tell them that they were earning more money now than they would ever make again. Some complained about anything. Real bloody Trogs. One got on his hind legs about escorting slow trucks, stating how he was not going to do this or that because they were driving so slowly and he would become a sitting duck. That was the job – shepherding trucks and trucks are by nature slow.

Although we had a choice of weapons, AK-47 or M4 carbine, I chose the latest-model M4 and a 9-millimetre double action pistol. A pistol is not a soldier's weapon. The Australians don't like them. Officers and leaders carried the bog-standard rifle or infantry weapon as it lowered the profile, making them look like an everyday digger. In Laos, I had a Colt Government 1911, and in Ireland the 9-millimetre Browning, and in Rhodesia first a Tokarev and later another Colt. The Colt and Browning, although different calibres, are both what is called single action. This new thing was the Beretta M9, a semi-automatic, 9mm, double-action pistol with a high-capacity magazine of 14 + 1 (in the chamber).

Golf Company's tasks were multi-faceted: covering humanitarian convoys, route reconnaissance, the security of leading travel and supply routes, escorting forensic scientists involved in uncovering war atrocities and mass graves. And lastly, to close with and destroy the enemy.

We would drive north of Mosul up to the Turkish border and pick up as many as seventy fuel trucks at a time and motor them south through Mosul. There were times after a contact or an IED incident that a call sign would be out on the road for twenty-six hours, especially if vehicles were damaged and we had to self-recover. There aren't too many ways you can get from the northern Turkish border down south. We would drive up and pull the convoy at a different hour, usually just before midnight or very early morning to try and get through the really hot areas where there was a high risk of contact. The infrastructure was abysmal; I mean there were only one or two roads you could travel. If the hadjis were patient you would have to pass them sometime. We came under fire with regular monotony from villages along the way. Our defence being soft-skinned with no armour, we were very fast, and we had crew-serviced weapons. At times, subject to the operation, we would go firm, or static, and fight. All routes and road junctions had a code name, but the choices were very limited. Every time we crossed a bridge running through Mosul, we came under fire from a certain minaret. In the end, they shot it to bits. I don't know if some Gurkha gunner did it or the Americans, but it had to come down. Mosques were more than just a pain to drive past; they were bloody dangerous. Halfway through one op in winter, I found after about two or three hours that my clothes were wet; had it not been so cold I wouldn't have felt it. At first, I thought maybe my water bottle had been punctured by a bullet during a firefight. When I got back to base, I learned that the previous team had taken fire, resulting in one member being shot through a leg artery and the only way they could clean out the vehicle fast enough before our call sign came on duty was to wash it out with buckets of water. Not only was I wet but my clothes were stained that brownie red colour.

We were detailed to travel to Tal Afar airbase, some sixty kilometres west of Mosul, along a route code-named Santa Fe. The USAF was flying recon flights every day and we would be on station so as soon as the reconnaissance plane touched down, the camera film would be offloaded from the recon plane, handed over to us, then we'd race over to the main airbase near Mosul and put it on a flight direct to the States and DC. There is only one road in and out of Tal Afar airbase, and only two choices once you hit town: you either go around the town or straight through it. Just outside of town you hit a service road that takes you the last ten clicks into the airbase. The reality was that, although this service road was mine-cleared every morning, it was the only route in – and out. That day our call sign picked up the film and left the airbase before being stopped at the security checkpoint. Right behind us three Stryker armoured personnel carriers pulled up. We cleared the security and headed down those ten clicks straight into an ambush. The platoon commander called for all cars to go firm and engage. The firefight had just started when down the street came the Strykers. They never even asked if they could join in: a sharp left turn off the road and straight through the hadjis' ambush, all guns blazing. Now, what was the chance of that?

I was to receive a letter of commendation and a certificate from the General Commanding US Forces Mosul. I am very proud of that fact and having worked for the US Forces. When I came out of Laos in 1968, I never even got a goodbye. At the end of Golf's contract, we had suffered five dead and forty-two wounded. No vehicle accidents and no deaths through NDs (negligent discharge of a firearm), all the statistics were combat-related. I must have been in the country for over nine months, and then the job ended. I would go on and sign another contract with a different company in 2007, but it was not the same. I began to wonder what I was doing here. I got an answer a short time later: the company lost the contract. I returned home. That was the last time I went to Iraq.

In what one would call my Iraq period I was to meet a woman named Judy B. On my first R&R I flew to the US and stayed with her. I had spent a lifetime in war and, consequently, almost every woman I had met lived in the country where I was fighting. Judy was an exception. She worked in Manhattan and was there when 9/11 went down. Apart from that, she was normal. Judy was a bright, talented woman and a director of a large American company. She was a single mother who had built a comfortable home and life for herself. I found her extremely interesting. In the past, she had researched works of art for buyers. She must have been good at it as that's how she bought her home. We spent hours talking about every subject under the sun. Judy was also a listener. I will always remember when she said that what you do does not define who you are. Judy showed me how to live and love again, and that life carries on. She helped put Humpty Dumpty together again. Then one day, I stopped counting the days and weeks since Barbara's death.

When I went back to Iraq, Judy was to buy a rifle and take shooting lessons. I set up a hunting trip for when I was back in Africa. Judy came to Africa, and we hunted together. She shot a very large warthog that had good ivory on it. I asked her why she shot a pig. She replied, 'It must be a Jewish thing.' That was good enough for me. I like uncomplicated. She is my friend. I still write to her but not as much as I used to. Now retired, she lives with her partner who used to fly helicopters. They moved to someplace warm. And me? No one gets cranky with a helicopter pilot having lived the life I have, so I am happy for them.

Doug found us a couple of good local contacts in Africa; non-disclosure agreements don't allow me to say much about them. I was working for a Chinese company along with Doug. We did two contracts planning and reconnoitring routes for hot extractions of Chinese nationals. Mostly we sat around waiting for the wheels to come off, something that often happens in Africa. If a contract came up, would I go? In all probability, yes, I would. It's no different now to what it was yesterday. Once I said I was just a special forces soldier, but time has taught me there is no such thing as just a special forces soldier. We are a unique breed. We will suffer extreme hardship, adversity and at times, death, to rescue one of our own. I still do training and shooting to keep my hand in. I am a divemaster, and I may become a diving instructor when I get time. Doug still loves dogs and picks up little birds when they fall out of the nests, and has an attitude deluxe, but he is working on it.

Some wars have to be fought; I am not anti-war. I have a problem with people who think they can kill and destroy little people like me, our families and way of life. They start wars to achieve their evil ends. The super elite by their own volition do exist and want to control everything. The globalists want a one-world government by 2030. I view them with the contempt they deserve. I miss the smell of cordite and earth-filled sandbags. The sounds of an AK or M4 have never left me. Until you have yelled, or heard someone yell, 'Contact, contact' you have never lived.

As mentioned, in one of my darker hours, Judy B told me what I do does not define who I am. There has to be more to that simple saying: 'If what we do does not define who we are', then where we come from or what we witness does not determine what we are, for if it does then my years of experience and watching a tormented bloody world have left me nothing more than a broken soldier. That's not to say …

Glossary

2IC	second in command
A-frame	Bergen rucksack
AK-47	Eastern bloc Avtomat-Kalashnikova 7.62 × 39 assault rifle
ANC	African National Congress.
AR7	derivative of Stoner's AR5 collapsible rifle, of .22 calibre
ball	British term for bullet; same as FMJ
BAR	Browning Automatic Rifle: not a rifle as such but a machine gun fed by a box magazine
Bingo line	aviation term, an imaginary line representing time or fuel burn that if crossed means you will not have enough fuel to return safely back to base
black stump	Australian term for back and beyond of anywhere, uninhabited
Browning	9mm pistol
carbine	M1 carbine, .30-calibre lightweight firearm (favoured by Asian troops due to its size)
casevac	casualty evacuation
CCB	Civil Cooperation Bureau. South African government-sponsored covert operation
chalk	British/Australian military term from WW2, a given number of paratroops who will board and exit an aircraft, i.e. a stick
cobber	Australian term for good mate/friend

cordite	a smokeless propellant used in bullets and shells
CPO	Close Protection Operator
CSI	Chief of Staff Intelligence
Cyclone	generic call sign for military aircraft (Rhodesian)
Cyclone 7	Alouette III helicopter (Rhodesian)
Dakota	C-47 transport aircraft, also converted DC-3s; Goony Bird (US slang)
desert boots	low ankle boots made of soft, light suede leather, ideal for hot sandy terrain
DZ	drop zone
FMJ	Full Metal Jacket – US ammunition/bullet
FOB	forward operational base
FRELIMO	Frente de Libertação de Moçambique/ Mozambique Liberation Front
Garda	the police service of the Republic of Ireland, from the Gaelic *Garda Síochána* (Guardians of the Peace)
G-car	Alouette III trooper/gunship
GI	a US soldier, der. Government/ General Issue
GPMG	general-purpose machine gun
GPS	Global Positioning System
hadji	slang for an Iraqi insurgent. der. *hajj*, the pilgrimage to Mecca
IED	improvised explosive device.
jammy	very fortunate, lucky (English slang)
JGs	jungle greens, Australian military uniform
kaffir	offensive term for a black African (Arabic der. *kafir* – infidel)
K-car	Alouette III gunship armed with a 20mm cannon (Rhodesian)
KIA	killed in action
LZ	landing zone
NATO 7.62	7.62 × 51-calibre NATO round

op/s	operation/s
POW	prisoner of war
PTSD	Post-Traumatic Stress Disorder
R&R	rest and recuperation
RENAMO	Resistência Nacional Moçambicana/ Mozambican National Resistance
RPD	Ruchnoy Pulemyot Degtyaryova 7.62mm machine gun
RPG	rocket-propelled grenade
Rupert	a derogatory term for a British officer
SACP	South African Communist Party
SADF	South African Defence Force
SAIMR	South African Institute for Maritime Research
SLR	self-loading rifle
Stoner/system	The AR-15 was developed in the late 1950s as a civilian weapon by Eugene Stoner, modified by the US military as the M16 Rifle. AR stands for the company ArmaLite (not automatic rifle)
T-28	North American Aviation Trojan aircraft
TRC	Truth and Reconciliation Commission (South African)
Trog	British soldier (slang), der. troglodyte
Uhuru	Freedom (Swahili)
UNITA	União Nacional para a Independência Total de Angola/The National Union for the Total Independence of Angola
USMC	United States Marine Corps
WOCS	War Office Controlled Stores
WRAC	Woman's Royal Army Corps